Contents

Introduction

MARRIAGE is Volume 316 in the **ISSUES** series. The aim of the series is to offer current, diverse information about important issues in our world, from a UK perspective.

ABOUT TITLE

According to a recent survey, the majority of people in the UK enjoy good quality relationships. This book, however, examines both the ups and downs. It looks at why people get married, or choose not to, the rights of cohabiting couples, the rise in relationship contracts and the difference between religious and civil marriages. It also considers the issues surrounding the topic of divorce, from how and why people get divorced to the ways in which they cope during and afterwards.

OUR SOURCES

Titles in the **ISSUES** series are designed to function as educational resource books, providing a balanced overview of a specific subject.

The information in our books is comprised of facts, articles and opinions from many different sources, including:

⇨ Newspaper reports and opinion pieces

⇨ Website factsheets

⇨ Magazine and journal articles

⇨ Statistics and surveys

⇨ Government reports

⇨ Literature from special interest groups.

A NOTE ON CRITICAL EVALUATION

Because the information reprinted here is from a number of different sources, readers should bear in mind the origin of the text and whether the source is likely to have a particular bias when presenting information (or when conducting their research). It is hoped that, as you read about the many aspects of the issues explored in this book, you will critically evaluate the information presented.

It is important that you decide whether you are being presented with facts or opinions. Does the writer give a biased or unbiased report? If an opinion is being expressed, do you agree with the writer? Is there potential bias to the 'facts' or statistics behind an article?

ASSIGNMENTS

In the back of this book, you will find a selection of assignments designed to help you engage with the articles you have been reading and to explore your own opinions. Some tasks will take longer than others and there is a mixture of design, writing and research-based activities that you can complete alone or in a group.

Useful weblinks

www.advicenow.org.uk

www.aviva.com

www.cafcass.gov.uk

www.childandfamilyblog.com

www.childline.org.uk

www.christianconcern.com

www.theconversation.com

www.divorce-online.co.uk

www.edp24.co.uk

www.familylaw.co.uk

www.familylives.org.uk

GOV.UK

www.theguardian.com

www.huffingtonpost.co.uk

www.humanism.org.uk

www.independent.co.uk

www.keystonelaw.co.uk

www.marilynstowe.co.uk

www.marriagefoundation.org.uk

www.nhs.uk

www.relate.org.uk

www.resolution.org.uk

www.separatedfamilies.info

www.telegraph.co.uk

www.yougov.co.uk

FURTHER RESEARCH

At the end of each article we have listed its source and a website that you can visit if you would like to conduct your own research. Please remember to critically evaluate any sources that you consult and consider whether the information you are viewing is accurate and unbiased.

Marriage

Series Editor: Cara Acred

Volume 316

Independence Educational Publishers

First published by Independence Educational Publishers

The Studio, High Green

Great Shelford

Cambridge CB22 5EG

England

ISBN-13: 978 1 86168 766 1

Printed in Great Britain

Zenith Print Group

The state of the UK's relationships

Following the publication of* The Way We Are Now *in 2014, Relate, Relationships Scotland and Marriage Care have once again commissioned a representative survey of over 6,000 people throughout the UK to profile the nation's relationships, offering a rich insight across five areas of our lives.

This unique survey offers us a glimpse of the home lives, working lives and sex lives of people in the UK and offers a perspective on the quality of our relationships with partners, families, friends and colleagues.

The Way We Are Now offers plenty to celebrate – the vast majority of people enjoy good quality relationships: 87% of people in couples are happy with their relationships; 71% of us enjoy good relationships with our colleagues; and nine out of ten of us report having close friends.

However, it also gives us an insight into the strains people face – with 61% of parents identifying money worries as a top strain on relationships; 22% of workers saying they work more hours than they want to and this damages

their health; and one in six people who are disabled or living with long-term health conditions reporting that they have no close friends.

For Relate, Relationships Scotland and Marriage Care this is a familiar picture. Our work with individuals, couples and families throughout the UK gives us first-hand experience of how people are working hard to stick together through good times and bad. And *The Way We Are Now* reflects these insights, including the results from a poll of over 450 of our relationship support practitioners.

Digging deeper, our findings tell a story about the interconnectedness of our lives, demonstrating why to consider relationships a purely private matter is to miss the point entirely. Issues traditionally considered to fall within the remit of public policy – such as the state of people's finances, conditions at work and provision for people who are disabled or living with long-term health conditions – have real impacts on our relationships. And conversely our relationships impact these realms – affecting our health, our well being and even our productivity at work. To that end, it's heartening that politicians, policy makers, and

commentators are increasingly recognising that relationships matter.

Relationships are our bedrock; they see us through the tough times. It's therefore good news that the majority of us enjoy good relationships with our partners, families, friends and colleagues.

However, as our survey shows, life can put up barriers to relationships – such as money worries and work pressures. And for some groups the barriers seem to be higher – with our findings in relation to people who are disabled or living with long-term health conditions offering particularly worrying insight.

When it comes to couple relationships, the majority of us understand the vital importance of communication and sharing problems, and we value commitment, and marriage as a sign of that commitment. And with the advent of equal marriage more of us are now free to choose to express our commitment in the way that suits us best.

However, we know our lives are built upon a rich patchwork of relationships and it's the quality of these relationships overall which will determine whether or not we thrive.

2015

⇨ The above information is reprinted with kind permission from Relate. Please visit www.relate.org.uk for further information.

Europe's marriage gap between rich and poor

By Harry Benson, Marriage Foundation and Spencer James, Brigham Young University

Across Europe, couples who don't marry are far more likely to split up than those who do, even after controls for age, education, religion, partner and parental divorce, and the presence of children (Dronkers, 2015).

The consequences of instability are far reaching for both adult and child outcomes. UK data, for example, shows that lone parents are seven times more likely than couple parents to rely on state benefits, and the children of lone parents are twice as likely to have problems with their health or at school (Maplethorpe et al, 2010).

Recent research from Marriage Foundation has also showed that marriage is increasingly the preserve of the rich. Among UK parents with children under five, 87% of those in the top income quintile were married compared to 24% in the bottom quintile (Benson & MacKay, 2015).

For this briefing note, we analysed data from the seventh round of the European Social Survey 2014, looking at the proportion of all parents with dependent children, and all adults, who were married.

Among parents and adults alike, a marriage gap exists between rich and poor throughout Europe. The same pattern found previously in the UK, by Benson & MacKay, was replicated in every one of the 20 European countries examined.

Poor parents were much less likely to be married than their rich counterparts. In some countries, marriage rates are higher still in the fourth income quintile.

This analysis shows that the trend away from marriage – and the relative stability that marriage provides – has barely affected the rich, but is strongly linked to lower income levels and, thus, the well being of adults, children, and the communities in which they reside.

The marriage gap

Our new data shows for the first time that the pattern of marriage among parents and all adults remains remarkably similar across Europe.

On average, 82% of parents in the highest income quintile are married compared to 42% of parents in the lowest income quintile.

Of the twenty countries examined – Spain, Germany, UK, France and Sweden – Sweden is unusual as the only country where marriage rates are actually lowest among parents in the second quintile.

In six of the twenty countries – Belgium, Israel, Lithuania, Norway, Slovenia, and Switzerland – the highest marriage rates were found in the fourth quintile.

However, across all 20 countries, marriage rates among rich parents were consistently higher than among poor parents.

Dividing countries into regions – Mediterranean, Scandinavia, Northern Europe, Eastern Europe – offers no distinctly regional characteristic of the marriage gap.

There appears to be as much variation within regions as between them.

The highest marriage gap overall is found in Denmark, where 81% of the richest parents are married, 3.9 times the level of 26% among the poorest parents.

Czech Republic comes a close second with a gap of 3.8 times between the 99% of rich parents and the 26% of poor parents who are married.

The marriage gap in Britain sits at 2.1 times, just above the European average of 1.9 times, where 84% of rich parents are married compared to 44% of poor parents.

The marriage gap is lowest in Slovenia, where the difference between rich and poor is 19% or 1.4 times, and Portugal, where the gap is 23% or also 1.4 times.

August 2016

⇨ The above information is reprinted with kind permission from Marriage Foundation. Please visit www.marriagefoundation.org.uk for further information.

We cater weddings to all budgets!
From 'the 'traditional', no expense spared.
To 'down at the local'. (beer and crisps provided)

Marriages and civil partnerships in the UK

Overview

You can get married or form a civil partnership in the UK if you're:

- 16 or over
- free to marry or form a civil partnership (single, divorced or widowed)
- not closely related.

You need permission from your parents or guardians if you're under 18 in England, Wales and Northern Ireland.

Only same sex couples can form a civil partnership.

There will be no change to the rights and status of EU nationals living in the UK, nor UK nationals living in the EU, while the UK remains in the EU.

Same sex couples

You can:

- form a civil partnership in England, Scotland, Wales and Northern Ireland
- get married in England, Scotland and Wales
- convert your civil partnership into a marriage in England, Scotland and Wales.

What you need to do

There are usually two steps to getting married or forming a civil partnership in England and Wales.

- Give notice at your local register office.
- Have a religious ceremony or civil ceremony at least 28 days after giving notice.

There may be different steps for some religious ceremonies.

Getting married or forming a civil partnership abroad

Find out about who to contact and which documents you may need to get from the UK authorities if you want to get married or form a civil partnership abroad.

Your overseas marriage or civil partnership will be recognised in the UK if you follow the correct process according to local law – you won't have to register it in the UK.

Marrying in England or Wales if you live abroad

You may be able to give notice in the country where you're living if that country has signed up to the 'British Subjects Facilities Acts'. Your partner must be a resident of England or Wales.

Contact the register office for the district in England and Wales where you intend to marry.

Countries signed up to the 'British Subjects Facilities Acts':

- Bahamas
- Barbados
- Belize
- Bermuda
- Botswana
- Canada (Newfoundland only)
- Cook Islands
- Cyprus
- Dominica
- Fiji
- The Gambia
- Ghana (former Gold Coast colony only)
- Gibraltar
- Grenada
- Guernsey (including Alderney)
- Isle of Man
- Jamaica
- Jersey
- Kiribati
- Kenya
- Leeward Islands
- Lesotho
- Malawi
- Malaysia (former Straits Settlement of Labuan, Malacca and Penang only)
- Mauritius
- Nauru
- New Zealand
- Nigeria
- Pitcairn Islands
- St Lucia
- St Vincent
- Seychelles
- Sierra Leone
- Solomon Islands
- Sri Lanka
- Swaziland
- Tanzania (Zanzibar only)
- Tonga
- Trinidad and Tobago
- Tuvalu
- Uganda
- Vanuatu
- Zambia
- Zimbabwe.

Giving notice at your local register office

For most marriages or civil partnerships you must give at least 28 full days' notice at your local register office.

You need to include details of where you intend to get married or form a civil partnership.

Your notice will be publicly displayed in the register office for 28 days.

You may also need to give notice here if you plan to marry or form a civil partnership abroad. Ask the overseas authority if you'll need a 'certificate of no impediment'.

Contact your local register office to make an appointment.

You can only give notice at a register office if you have lived in the registration district for at least the past seven days.

There are different rules for religious ceremonies.

You must get married or register your civil partnership within one year, or three months if you're in Scotland.

Foreign nationals

There are different rules if you or your partner are a foreign national from outside the European Economic Area (EEA) or Switzerland.

Documents to take to the register office

When you go to the register office, you need to take proof of your name, age and nationality. For example your:

⇨ valid passport

⇨ birth certificate

⇨ national identity card from the European Economic Area (EEA) or Switzerland

⇨ certificate of registration

⇨ certificate of naturalisation

⇨ biometric residence card or permit

⇨ travel document.

If you've changed your name, you must bring proof – e.g. a copy of a deed poll.

The registrar also needs proof of your address, for example a:

⇨ valid UK or EEA driving licence

⇨ gas, water or electricity bill from the last three months

⇨ bank or building society statement from the last month

⇨ council tax bill from the last 12 months

⇨ mortgage statement from the last 12 months

⇨ current tenancy agreement

⇨ letter from your landlord confirming you live there and including your landlord's name, address and their signature dated within the last seven days

Check with your local register office if they require a photo ID

You might need other documents if you don't have a valid passport and you were born after 1983 – check with the register office.

You each need to pay a £35 fee when you attend the register office to give notice. It can be more if you or your partner are from outside EEA or Switzerland.

If you've been divorced or widowed

If you've been married or in a civil partnership before, you need to take either:

⇨ a decree absolute or final order

⇨ the death certificate of your former partner.

A foreign divorce will usually be recognised in England and Wales if it was valid in the country where it took place.

The registrar will check your overseas divorce documents and may have to get in touch with the General Register Office to confirm whether your marriage or civil partnership can go ahead.

Religious ceremonies

A religious wedding can take place at a church, chapel or other registered religious building.

Religious blessing can take place after a civil ceremony in a register office.

You can't get married in an Anglican Church as a same sex couple. You can get married in other religious buildings if:

⇨ the religious organisation allows the marriage of same sex couples to take place

⇨ the premises have been registered for the marriage of same sex couples.

Anglican marriages

To get married in an Anglican church, contact your local church in:

⇨ England

⇨ Wales.

You don't usually need to give notice with the register office if you're getting married in an Anglican church and both you and your partner are:

⇨ British citizens

⇨ from the European Economic Area (EEA) or Switzerland.

Officials performing Anglican marriages will register your marriage.

You need to give notice at a register office if you or your partner are from outside the EEA or Switzerland.

Jewish and Quaker marriages

You need to give notice with the register office at least 28 days before the ceremony. Officials performing Jewish or Quaker marriages will register marriages.

Non-Anglican Christian marriages and all other religions

You need to give notice with the register office at least 28 days before the ceremony.

Authorised officials, including ministers and priests of other religions, can register marriages.

You must give notice at a 'designated' register office if you or your partner are from outside the EEA or Switzerland.

Weddings and civil partnership ceremonies

Vows

You must exchange some formal wording if you're getting married.

Discuss any other wording you want in the ceremony with the person conducting it.

You don't need to exchange vows for a civil partnership, but you can do so if you wish.

Civil ceremonies can include readings, songs or music, but must not include anything that's religious, e.g. hymns or readings from the Bible.

You'll need to have at least two witnesses at the ceremony.

Signing the register

You, your partner and your two witnesses must sign the marriage register or civil partnership document.

Cost of registering a marriage or civil partnership

You have to pay a fee to register a UK marriage or civil partnership – different fees may apply abroad.

This is £46 if you have the ceremony at a register office, but may be more at other venues. Ask the registrar or religious minister for details.

The marriage or civil partnership certificate costs £4 on the day of the event or £10 after. You may need a copy to prove your marital status in the future.

Venues

You can have a civil ceremony or civil partnership at:

⇨ a register office

- any venue approved by the local council, e.g. a stately home or hotel
- a religious premises where permission has been given by the organisation and the premises approved by the local authority.

The Home Office has a list of all approved civil marriage and civil partnership venues.

10 April 2017

- The above information is reprinted with kind permission from GOV. UK.

Religious vs civil marriage: untangling the knot

By Marilyn Stowe

Say the word 'wedding' to most Brits and you can be pretty sure it will bring certain images to mind: walking down the aisle, the bride in white arm in arm with her father, a vicar waiting for the happy couple with a wry smile. In other words: a church wedding – I think it is fair to say that is the default image in most people's minds.

The details differ, of course, for those from certain backgrounds. The particulars and traditions of Jewish, Muslim and Hindu weddings are all distinct but the fundamental message is the same: getting married is a religious as much as a social and legal event.

But of course that is not necessarily the case. It is perfectly legal in this country to turn marriage into an entirely civil affair by marrying in a registry office, although even then, marriage is given a unique status through the compulsory exchange of vows. It is this element, more perhaps than any other, that distinguishes marriage from civil partnership and which arguably fuelled the drive towards the legalisation of same sex marriage. Civil partnerships convey the same rights but are essentially a form-filling affair, lacking the special ceremonial allure and magic of marriage. It was no surprise to me or many others that same sex couples would want the latter too.

You can marry in hotels and similar venues provided these have been approved by the local authority. Sadly, for the more adventurous amongst us, it is not legal to marry in the open air in England, by a waterfall or in a flowery meadow, unless the happy couple also conduct a legal ceremony in a 'fixed' structure licensed for the purpose.

Oddly, this is not the case, however, in Scotland or Northern Ireland!

Yesterday, I received an interesting question from a reader of the blog. A gentleman calling himself 'urtly' wrote to ask:

"Hello, I want to ask because it is not very clear to me yet.

"I have done a wedding ceremony in the UK in a Pentecostal church but has never registered my marriage, after one year she have abandon me. I always thought that the marriage is not valid so I moved abroad to a Dutch Caribbean Island.

"Overhear I have med a young lady and we have married, but now she is stating, that what I am doing is polygamy and that I can face the jail and that she wants her divorce. She wants me to go and divorce the other lady first and then come back to get married with her. Because she is a Christian. But where does she wants me to go and divorce that lady while we have never registered our wedding.

"Can you please help me and tell me the truth, if my first wedding ceremony was legal to the UK law or I am not legally married and can not face jail sentenced over hear in this Island.

"Hope to hear very soon of you."

I thought urtly's dilemna raised several interesting points.

At heart, marriage is a legal contract and signing the certificate a civil process. That's why it's perfectly legal to tie the knot in a registry office and go away just as married as the participants in a full white wedding. But in recognition of tradition, special dispensation is made for some religious traditions.

As establishment organisations, the Churches of England and Wales both have the automatic right to conduct legally valid marriages without the involvement of a registry office, as long as both parties are residents of countries in the EU. If not, then 28 days' notice must be given.

At this point, things start to get a little more complicated. Ministers and priests of other Christian denominations, as well as rabbis, imams, and representatives of other religions are not given an automatic right to conduct weddings that can dispense with the need for civil registrations and need to apply for this.

For Jewish and Quaker weddings, authorisation is given as a matter of course, but this is not the case with other churches and religions, including Pentecostalism, where authorisation may or may not be given. If it is not, then one of two things must happen: either a registrar must attend the ceremony to legalise it, or the happy couple will have to attend the registry office separately, before or after the ceremony, to sign the forms.

So we cannot know for sure, without a little more information, whether urtly's wedding was legally valid in the UK. If he believes it was not, it is unlikely he and his first wife attended a registry office or a registrar attended the wedding. But it is just possible that the Pentecostal Minister had authorisation.

If he did not, then it is likely that urtly's marriage was invalid under English law – or to use legal terminology, a 'nullity', something that never achieved legal validity in the first place. He could apply in the English courts for a 'decree of nullity', certifying the maybe-marriage's lack of validity – once he has established that, of course.

But there's another question to be asked here: what is the legal situation in his new home? How does the law of this Dutch Caribbean island view marriages like his first, which may be null and void? I would advise him to investigate as soon as he can and seek legal advice if at all possible. What do the authorities on his sunny new home need him to do, if anything, in order to ensure his second marriage is fully recognised and legally valid?

I wish him the best of luck.

1 June 2016

⇨ The above information is reprinted with kind permission from Marilyn Stowe. Please visit http://www.marilynstowe.co.uk/2016/06/01/religious-vs-civil-marriage-untangling-the-knot/ for further information.

© Marilyn Stowe 2017

Humanist weddings continue to surge in number, bucking national trend

The British Humanist Association (BHA) has called for legal recognition to be given to humanist weddings across the UK, as new national marriage figures in England and Wales show that marriages overall have declined in number at the same time as non-legal humanist weddings have surged in popularity.

The Office of National Statistics (ONS) has announced that the number of marriage ceremonies in England and Wales declined by 8.6% in 2013. Meanwhile BHA-accredited celebrants in England, Wales and Northern Ireland performed 26% more weddings in 2013 than in 2012 – growth that has continued since, with 87% more being performed in 2015 than 2012.

The number of humanist weddings performed in Scotland has grown exponentially since their legal recognition as marriages, reversing the overall decline in the number of marriages in Scotland. In 2010 Humanist Society Scotland (HSS) performed more marriages than the Catholic Church, and in 2013 it performed more than double. It is expected to have overtaken the Church of Scotland in 2015 to become the largest provider of belief-based weddings. Humanist marriages in Scotland were legalised in 2005, since which time the number of such weddings has gone from about 50 per year to well over 4,000.

It is still not possible to have a legally recognised humanist marriage elsewhere in the UK. In England and Wales, the UK Government is currently considering whether such recognition should be given. In Northern Ireland there is no government consideration of the issue. The BHA is today calling for legal recognition across the whole UK.

BHA Head of Ceremonies Isabel Russo commented, "The UK Government says it is in favour of marriage as an institution. If that is true then there is one easy, legitimate step it can take to massively boost the number of couples getting married, and that is extending legal recognition to humanist marriages in England and Wales.

"We will be continuing to work to see the Government make use of its power to extend such recognition as we know that such a change would be overwhelmingly popular, simple to introduce, and grant the same freedoms to humanist couples that are already enjoyed by religious couples."

Wouldn't it be great to start your married life with a ceremony that really means something? To tell your friends and family what your relationship means to you, and why you are choosing to get married?

Many of us who aren't religious are looking for a wedding that is more flexible and personal than a civil or register office ceremony.

Humanist, non-religious wedding ceremonies may not yet have full legal recognition in all parts of the UK, but they do give you the opportunity to mark your marriage where you want, when you want and how you want. You can find out more on the Humanist Ceremonies website.

28 April 2016

⇨ The above information is reprinted with kind permission from the British Humanist Association. Visit humanism.org.uk for further information.

© British Humanist Association 2017

Why have a church wedding if you haven't a shred of Christian belief?

A wedding invitation made me sigh this week – because the wedding's taking place in church.

Yes, of course for many believers it's the only place and the perfect place. Others, while not churchgoers, want to make the most important promise of their lives in an important and sacred place, I can see that.

But the rest? Why?

I love a wedding – all that optimism – and I'm lucky over the years to have been to some amazing church weddings, some humble, some incredibly posh but all very special, so that it's been a privilege to be part of them.

Such as my cousin's wedding that was half in English, half in Welsh and we nearly raised the rafters of the tiny church when we sang Calon Lan at full pelt before piling out to the pub across the road.

Or the wedding of two old friends, both widowed, marrying in their sixties. There were no hymns and just a handful of us there and it was incredibly moving.

I've also been to a few that have been downright uncomfortable.

Clue: church weddings include prayers and generally, hymns. For a lot of people that's a foreign country.

Now most schools no longer have a hymn-singing, praying daily assembly, people don't know the drill. They don't know what to do. At best, they feel uncomfortable, at worst they make everyone else feel that way too.

The organist playing doggedly a virtual solo through three verses of All Things Bright and Beautiful or Morning Has Broken is bad enough, while a handful of us try to sing and the rest of the congregation shuffles and coughs and wonders how soon it will be over.

Sometimes the congregation seem to be there to be entertained and consider the vicar as some sort of compere, presiding over a glorified game show where everyone has to have a good laugh.

The worst was a wedding where, when the vicar asked the bride "Will you take William to be your husband? Will you love him, comfort him, honour and protect him, forsaking all others…"

The bride giggled and replied "Oooh, can I think about that one?" and turned to the laughing congregation for applause.

The priest sighed and smiled through gritted teeth.

The church wants to welcome us all, of course. Anyway, I suppose weddings are a business and the church is in business just like anyone else and they're not going to turn folk away.

Churches are beautiful, impressive buildings, but if you haven't a shred of Christian belief, there are plenty of other equally beautiful buildings where you can get married.

Anyway, we shall go to this wedding with good heart and good voice – and just hope we won't be the only people singing…

23 January 2017

⇨ The above information is reprinted with kind permission from the *Eastern Daily Press*. Please visit www.edp24.co.uk for further information.

"Some people don't like the phrase man and wife" – the campaign for equal civil partnerships

There are lots of straight couples who don't want to get married but worry about the financial and legal risks of cohabiting. Extending civil partnerships could be one answer – and the pressure is growing.

I can't recall when my partner and I agreed we wouldn't get married. It may have come up in discussions about our home lives: her parents had had an unpleasant divorce when she was young, which rather ruined the romance of marriage; my unmarried parents had had a rather pleasant separation, which left me unsure as to the point of the institution in general.

Over the years, though, this abstract opposition to marriage has become more concrete. Buying a (shared-ownership) house forced us to ask why we didn't want the legal protections of marriage, to go with the intertwining of our lives in other respects. We were named in each others' wills, paid bills and rent from a joint bank account and owned a house in common: why not make it all official?

Part of the answer was that the tradition of marriage remained a turn-off. For me, its history is hard to ignore: a woman may not have to swear "to obey" any more, but the institution remains the same. Symbolism is a powerful thing, and it's not something an individual can erase at will. My partner has her own objection: she doesn't want to be a wife, a word with a loaded history.

We aren't alone. Many people are turning their back on marriage, choosing to cohabit without any formal legal partnership, or cobbling together the best they can with a mixture of contract law, trust law and hope. For some, such as my parents, this works: their separation didn't come with years of legal wrangling, and the balance of power in their relationship was largely equal.

But it can also come with risks. Such couples have no protections, responsibilities or bonds, beyond those they have explicitly put in place. There

is, contrary to popular belief, no such thing as a "common law marriage," a fact that many only discover when it's too late. "There is no better protection than what marriage gives people," says Shlomit Glaser, a family law expert at solicitors Glaser Jones Law. "Because historically, that was the reason for marriage: to give protection, usually to the wife, and define the obligation of the husband."

Without legal protection, a relationship that turns sour can become extremely damaging. "I had a situation where a woman ended up without heating in her house when her partner said he wouldn't pay for it," Glaser says.

Cohabiting couples are slowly gaining some rights. In early February, a landmark supreme court case ruled that cohabitees are automatically entitled to the pensions of their deceased partners, even if they are not explicitly nominated as a beneficiaries. But it's unlikely that there will ever be an automatic bundle of rights for unmarried partners. That could pose a problem, with people accidentally burdening themselves with inalienable responsibilities purely by moving in with a loved one. Glaser suggests that a piecemeal approach to the problem, amending specific bills such as those governing inheritance or taxation, would allow for the most glaring injustices to be rectified without introducing new problems.

There's another potential solution, though. The UK already has a legal construct that provides a couple with the same rights as in marriage, while dispensing with the potentially distasteful symbolism. The downside is that it's only available if both partners are the same sex.

Civil partnerships were introduced in 2004, as a compromise short of

legislating for same-sex marriage. Almost immediately, a campaign was launched to allow mixed-sex couples to obtain civil partnerships, but it contained an element of legal trickery: the hope was that a ruling that civil partnerships were discriminatory would set a precedent that could open up marriage to same-sex couples.

With the passage of the Marriage (Same Sex Couples) Act in 2013, that motivation was rendered moot. Yet the campaign for mixed-sex civil partnerships continued. Nine months after the first same-sex marriage ceremonies took place, Rebecca Steinfeld and Charles Keidan launched a judicial review after being turned away from Chelsea town hall, where they had tried to register a civil partnership. After years of legal wrangling, the Royal Courts of Justice are set to hand down a judgment on the matter on Tuesday.

Steinfeld and Keidan's case quickly attracted supporters, and grew into the campaign group Equal Civil Partnerships. Matt Hawkins, the group's campaign manager, argues that a change in the law would provide the perfect model for people like me and my partner. "There's a whole constituency of people out there who don't like marriage," he says. "They don't like the phrase 'man and wife', and don't like the patriarchal implications, but they do want the legal benefits."

It would be a surprisingly easy change to institute. The Conservative MP Tim Loughton, who has introduced a bill in parliament aimed at equalising civil partnerships, told the House of Commons in January: "All that is required is a simple one-line amendment to the Civil Partnership Act 2004." The substantive section of Loughton's bill comes to just 25 words.

"Part 1 of the Civil Partnership Act 2004 is amended as follows: In Section 1, subsection (1), leave out 'of the same sex'." That's it.

But there is opposition. In the Commons, the minister for apprenticeships and skills, Robert Halfon, argued that Loughton's amending bill could have "unknown, untested effects on myriad legislation-spanning areas such as pensions, devolution, international recognition, gender recognition, adultery and consummation", arguing, in effect, that the work wasn't worth it for a minor change. Others have been more forthright: when the issue was broached during the debates around same-sex marriage, David Cameron argued that such a change could "weaken" marriage.

It's difficult to respond. On the one hand, marriage seems far more weakened by forcing it upon couples who don't believe in the institution. On the other, international evidence suggests that civil partnerships could be surprisingly popular.

The French equivalent to civil partnerships is called the civil solidarity pact (*pacte civil de solidarité*, or Pacs). Like British civil partnerships, its roots lie in an attempt to satisfy demands from same-sex couples for equal marriage; unlike civil partnerships, it was solidly second-tier, with lesser tax benefits and property rights matched by a simpler process for separation.

Despite this, they have proved remarkably popular for couples of mixed and same genders: in 2015, according to the French national statistics board Insee, 188,900 couples entered into a Pacs, compared with 236,400 couples who got married. Marriage figures have declined by a fifth in a little more than a decade, and it looks as if most of those couples are getting Pacs instead. It's not all bad for defenders of traditional marriage, though: more than 40% of Pacs unions that end do so because the couple decide to get married.

There is one place in the British Isles where mixed-sex couples can get civil partnerships: the Isle of Man. In July 2016, the crown dependency legalised same-sex marriage, and went one step further by also legalising mixed-sex civil partnerships.

Adeline Cosson and Kieran Hodgson, the first mixed-sex couple to get one

on the island, said that they wanted to "keep it simple" rather than have a traditional wedding, but didn't rule out getting married at a later date – a reminder that not everyone who wants a civil partnership is opposed to marriage itself.

Despite the island's close ties to the UK, Manx civil partnerships aren't recognised by the British Government unless they are between same-sex couples, but that hasn't stopped mixed-sex couples making the three-hour boat trip from Liverpool – or 80-minute flight from London – to get one. Martin Loat and Claire Beale were the first such couple from the UK, and the second on the island, to register their partnership.

"We've never really been the marrying types," says Loat. "We don't feel it's necessary to take a vow or publicly pledge in any form to validate our relationship." He and Beale travelled to the island in the hope that their partnership would be a small addition to the pressure on the UK to legislate for equality.

There is another constituency with a voice worth hearing on the matter: the LGBT community, for whom civil partnerships were created in the first place. Ben Summerskill, director of the Criminal Justice Alliance, was chief executive of Stonewall from 2003 to 2014, and was instrumental in the fight for civil partnerships and equal marriage.

By and large, he says, he wants to stay out of the debate. "My view is that it's really for straight people to decide whether they want them, and it's not for me to go round instructing straight people what's good for them." Nonetheless, he acknowledges that gay people may have a reason for speaking up. Many, for instance, still choose to get civil partnerships, despite the option of marriage being available.

"I think the reason for that is that there were quite a lot of gay people who feel that they waited an incredibly long time for this, and finally had something that was slightly special, and certainly recognised their existence," he says. Their importance as a tool of gay visibility, even today, shouldn't be underestimated: "Suddenly, on the income tax form, it said 'marriage or civil partnerships'. Within five years almost everyone in this country knew someone

who was in a civil partnership, or had been to a celebration, and all of them were just like all the weddings everyone has been to."

Hawkins, of the Equal Civil Partnerships campaign, acknowledges this argument. But, he says, "What we want to be about is treating love, and couples, entirely as equals. Everyone's relationship is special. But if it's seen as good enough for same-sex couples, it should be good enough for mixed-sex couples."

I would like a civil partnership, but unlike Hawkins, Steinfeld and Keidan, I haven't spent my life campaigning for it. I do worry it could undercut the years that LGBT activists spent arguing civil partnerships were an offensive half-measure on the road to true equality. It's also true that many of the issues of remaining unmarried can be countered on a piecemeal basis, with contracts and undertakings. But just as I don't want my romantic life to have a seal of approval from the state, to have to 'take' someone as my 'wife', I also don't want it to devolve into a mountain of paperwork just to ensure I can visit my partner in hospital if the worst happens.

Because of that possibility, I'm grateful to the campaign for pushing for my rights, and for those of so many others. If the Royal Courts of Justice rejects Steinfeld and Keidan's case, that's not the end of the matter: Loughton's bill offers hope, and even the Government has suggested reviewing the law at some point.

But if all that fails – well, then my bluff has been called. Is it really that I don't like the implications of a traditional service, the outdated terminology, and the long history of patriarchy looming over the whole thing? Or am I just afraid of commitment? Hopefully, I'll find out sooner rather than later.

20 February 2017

⇨ The above information is reprinted with kind permission from *The Guardian*. Please visit www.theguardian.com for further information.

Humanists in England and Wales call for legal humanist weddings as Scottish Parliament officially recognises humanist ceremonies for marriage provision in law

Thousands of humanists in England and Wales have been calling on the Government to give legal recognition to humanist weddings this Valentine's Day, while in Scotland the Scottish Parliament has officially recognised Humanist Society Scotland (HSS) as the first non-religious organisation with a permanent right in law to conduct legal marriages under the 1977 Marriage Act.

Humanist weddings were first recognised in Scotland 11 years ago. Since then, the popularity of humanist weddings has skyrocketed, with more than 4,200 humanist ceremonies taking place in 2015 alone. In England and Wales, humanist wedding ceremonies continue to have no legal recognition despite the British Humanist Association (BHA) taking more weddings each year than most recognised religious organisations. The BHA conducts over 1,000 humanist weddings a year, with most couples then having a simple signing at the register office in order become legally married. A YouGov survey in 2016 found that roughly 15 million Brits had been to a humanist ceremony.

Powers secured in the Marriage Act 2013 allow the UK Government to give legal recognition to humanist weddings in England and Wales should it choose to. However, following a public consultation which showed overwhelming support for legalisation and a subsequent Law Commission review, there has been no action. Over the past few months, thousands of humanists from across England and Wales have written to their MPs calling for humanist weddings to be given legal recognition after years of inaction from the Government.

Isabel Russo, Head of Ceremonies at the BHA, commented: "The Scottish Parliament should be commended for responding to the growing numbers of humanists across the UK and recognising their equal right to be married in accordance with their deepest held values and beliefs. The popularity of humanist marriages is undeniable: humanist weddings are now the most popular form of belief-based marriage on offer in Scotland and they continue to surge in popularity in England and Wales. Humanist Society Scotland becoming the first ever non-religious body prescribed in law to conduct marriages is further testament to the high standards of celebrants trained accredited by longstanding humanist organisations.

"Non-religious couples have been badly let down in England and Wales in having to have separate humanist and then civil ceremonies, and many have started making the trip over to Scotland specifically in order to have a legal humanist wedding. This Valentine's Day, when millions across the UK will be popping the question and hoping for a perfect wedding that reflects their love and commitment, we would urge the Lord Chancellor to act decisively and at last give humanist weddings in England and Wales the recognition they deserve, so that humanist couples across Britain can enjoy the same rights afforded to religious couples."

Notes

For further comment or information, please contact BHA Director of Public Affairs and Policy Pavan Dhaliwal on pavan@humanism.org.uk or 0773 843 5059.

Read more about the BHA campaign on marriage reform at https://humanism.org.uk/campaigns/human-rights-and-equality/marriage-laws/.

About the change in Scots law

The new regulation has been made using a Scottish Statutory Instrument (SSI) under section 8(1)(a)(ii) and (1B)(a)(i) of the Marriage (Scotland) Act 1977(1) and section 94A(1)(a)(i) of the Civil Partnership Act 2004(2) (Amendment of the Civil Partnership (Prescribed Bodies) (Scotland) Regulations 2016). The SSI is available to view online at: http://www.legislation.gov.uk/ssi/2016/427/contents/made.

HSS will be the first body to be added to the list of prescribed bodies since 1977, and the first ever non-religious organisation. The other organisations prescribed since 1977 are: The Baptist Union of Scotland; The Congregational Union of Scotland; The Episcopal Church (etc.); The Free Church of Scotland; The Free Presbyterian Church of Scotland; The Hebrew Congregation; The Methodist Church in Scotland; The Religious Society of Friends; The Roman Catholic Church; The Salvation Army; The Scottish Unitarian Association, and The United Free Church of Scotland. (Ministers of the Church of Scotland are entitled to conduct weddings without being a prescribed body.)

The British Humanist Association is the national charity working on behalf of non-religious people who seek to live ethical and fulfilling lives on the basis of reason and humanity. It promotes a secular state and equal treatment in law and policy of everyone, regardless of religion or belief.

14 February 2017

⇨ The above information is reprinted with kind permission from the British Humanist Association. Please visit www.humanism.org.uk for further information.

Discrimination against same-sex couples denied religious marriage is endemic, says York academic

New research by academics at the Universities of York and Leeds highlights the prevailing extent of discrimination against same-sex couples wanting religious marriage ceremonies.

Professor Paul Johnson, from York's Department of Sociology, has examined the legal framework in England and Wales that allows religious organisations to refuse to marry same-sex couples.

Working in collaboration with Professor Robert Vanderbeck at Leeds, Professor Johnson found that same-sex couples are excluded from approximately 40,200 places of worship in which opposite-sex couples can get married.

Same-sex couples are not permitted to marry in any of the 17,350 churches of the Church of England and the Church in Wales, or in nearly 23,000 other places of worship, such as Roman Catholic churches, Islamic mosques, and Hindu temples.

Although same-sex marriage has been legal in England and Wales since 2014, religious organisations are under no obligation to extend their marriage services to gay couples.

Opt-in decision

The Marriage (Same Sex Couples) Act 2013 provides the means for organised religions – other than the Church of England – to opt in to conduct same-sex marriages, with the decision left to individual institutions.

Only 139 places of worship are registered to perform same-sex marriage in England and Wales, meaning approximately 99.5 per cent do not offer it. Just 23 same-sex couples had a religious marriage ceremony in 2014, compared with over 68,000 opposite-sex couples.

Professor Paul Johnson said: "The level of discrimination is staggering. If you are a same-sex couple in England and Wales then you most likely live in a town where there is no opportunity to have a religious marriage ceremony. That means you are completely shut out of a mainstream cultural practice that opposite-sex couples take for granted.

"Recent reports describe same-sex couples 'shunning' religious wedding ceremonies, but the reality is they are simply being denied the opportunity. Parliament has agreed a legislative framework for marriage that is allowing extensive discrimination, and the figures support this."

Minor faith groups

Professor Robert Vanderbeck said: "Because none of the mainstream religious faiths will marry same-sex couples, such couples need to rely on minor faith groups, such as Unitarians, to be willing to marry them. The problem is, the couple might not share that faith."

Church of England Canon law - which defines marriage as the 'union of one man with one woman' – co-exists alongside the contrary general marriage statute law allowing same-sex marriage, due to the religious protections included in the 2013 Act.

3 May 2017

⇨ The above information is reprinted with kind permission from the University of York. Please visit www.york.ac.uk for further information.

Could ten-year relationship contracts replace life-long marriage?

One in four marriages ends in divorce.

By Rachel Moss

One in four marriages carried out in the UK ends in divorce, so could it be time to shake up the way we commit to our partner?

Some relationship experts have suggested engaging in a ten-year "relationship contract" could be a better way to ensure your relationship stands the test of time.

The idea is that couples should set out their expectations of what their relationship will be like, as well as detail what will happen financially if they break up.

After nine years, the couple should re-evaluate their contract, deciding whether they are still on track or making changes in their love life where necessary.

Sex and relationship expert Dr Nikki Goldstein believes a ten-year relationship contract, or a ten-year marriage contract, could help couples work through their problems.

"I see people all the time that are clinging on to marriages because that's easier, or the idea of being on your own or divorced is scary," she told Daily Mail Australia.

"They don't want to be seen to be failing, but they never stop to think 'why isn't it working for us?'

"If there was more social acceptance from society and we did have more encouragement to create our own rules and marriages, maybe we'd see a decrease in the amount of divorces."

Writer and HuffPost UK blogger Sarah Tinsley has welcomed the concept, saying relationship contracts may enable couples to maintain "an equal balance of power in the relationship".

"Marriage is still very biased towards the male partner assuming control, even if you try to have a 'modern' marriage," she told HuffPost UK.

"Allowing both partners the same input, without the historical baggage of a wedding, certainly permits both parties to start on an even footing."

According to Tinsley, such a contract would also encourage couples to re-evaluate "what a successful long-term partnership actually looks like" and acknowledge "that people change over time".

"Assuming that everything will be fine after you've said 'I do' can limit the amount of reflection that happens as you progress," she said.

"Formalising this process through a contract might seem 'unromantic' to some, but it could well lead to more honest, balanced and successful relationships."

In contrast, Keelie Briggs, founder of the wedding planning site Wedding It Your Way, does not believe ten-year contracts are a good idea.

"I prefer a traditional marriage and believe if you choose to commit to someone, you do so because you know that the love you feel for them has no time limits," she said.

"A marriage 'contract' seems more of a business agreement made out of convenience than a declaration of love and devotion as a marriage should be."

Peter Saddington, a counsellor at relationship's charity Relate, said all forms of long-term relationships take commitment and hard work.

"Whether it's a marriage, living together or a ten-year contract, it makes sense to evaluate your relationship along the way to make sure you're both happy with how things are going," he told HuffPost UK.

"Important life events – like having a baby, a death in the family or retirement – can put a strain on couple relationships and that's often when people come to Relate."

He added that there's "no need to wait" until a problem arises to seek relationship support.

"Taking the time to check in on how you're both feeling will help to make your relationship as strong as possible for when life throws you a curve ball," he said.

"Of course, many couples end up having children and that's a life-long commitment whether you're together or not.

"Parents have a responsibility to ensure they're doing the best for their children as they grow up, including making the family relationships around them as strong as possible."

6 December 2016

⇨ The above information is reprinted with kind permission from The Huffington Post UK. Please visit www.huffingtonpost.co.uk for further information.

The majority of wedding traditions are still popular, but don't ask the bride's family to pay

Whilst very few think the bride should agree to obey her husband, most people also don't think she should get to speak at her reception.

Weddings are a joyous occasion, and people seem to be particularly fond of many of their traditional aspects. Of 12 wedding traditions surveyed by YouGov, seven traditions were still favoured by more than half of people. The most popular wedding traditions are the groom having a best man (78%), the bride and groom's first dance (75%) and the best man's speech (73%).

People were only in favour of dropping three wedding traditions. The bride's family paying for the wedding was the most unpopular, with 76% saying it should be dropped against 9% saying it should be preserved. Indeed, the majority of people (56%) feel that the bride and groom should bear the main cost of the wedding, followed by both sets of parents (30%).

The other two wedding traditions people would like to see dropped are the bride promising to obey her husband (70% of all respondents, and 80% of women), and giving out wedding favours to guests (42%).

The speeches at wedding receptions are traditionally a male-dominated affair. The groom, best man and the father of the bride all expected to make a speech, and people seem to be broadly happy with this arrangement. Six in ten (62%) believe the best man should give a speech, as well as 51% for the groom and 48% for the father of the bride. Despite the increasing popularity of the bride giving a speech, though, just 16% of people think that she should.

Indeed, this view is just as widely held among women as men. Women are actually more likely than men to want the best man, groom and father of the bride to speak (particularly those last two – possibly because men can imagine themselves having to give that speech and don't want to), and are marginally less likely to think that the bride should speak than men.

Common wedding dilemmas for couples...

The survey reveals attitudes on common dilemmas that many engaged couples may face in planning their wedding.

Starting from the very earliest point in the wedding process, the most accepted time for a couple to be together before getting engaged is between six months and two years, according to 57% of people. Being together for at least a year is the most popular choice, with 27%, followed by at least two years (18%) and at least six months (12%). Women are slightly more likely than men to favour a longer run-up, with 56% thinking couples should wait for at least a year, compared to 50% of men.

In terms of picking a date, couples will be pleased to find they are afforded plenty of flexibility, with the vast majority (87%) of people thinking that it is acceptable to have a wedding on a weekday.

Opinion is split on which guests should be allowed to bring children to a wedding. Three in ten (29%) think that only children of close friends and family should be allowed to attend. A further 25% think that all guests should be allowed to bring children, whilst 21% think that only children of close family should be allowed. Only 9% of people think that children shouldn't be allowed at all.

Knowing whether to invite younger children can present a more complex dilemma, with the potential for the ceremony to be disrupted by noise. Couples should be aware that slightly more people would prefer for children under the age of six to be able to attend rather than be excluded (40% vs 36%).

In terms of getting invitations sent, most people would prefer to receive a wedding invitation by post (61%). A further 26% don't care one way or the other, whilst only 3% would prefer some sort of online or email invitation. They also feel it is perfectly acceptable for the couple to register a list of wedding presents (74%) or to ask for money instead (59%).

...and for guests

Likewise, the survey also provides help for wedding attendees. Should a couple send a wedding invitation with no information or guidance on presents, the majority of people opt to either: give money to the couple (28%), give a gift voucher (26%) or a boxed present (21%). Similarly, if the wedding invitation doesn't provide information on bringing a plus one, the majority (52%) of people believe this means that you should not bring a guest.

10 August 2016

⇨ The above information is reprinted with kind permission from YouGov. Please visit www.yougov.co.uk for further information.

Prenups: only for the rich?

By Hilary Pennington-Mellor, Family & Matrimonial, Probate & Estate Planning

The notion of a prenup can conjur up images of wealthy spouses seeking to protect holiday homes in the Bahamas or sprawling, countryside mansions. But these types of agreements are fast becoming a popular choice, across the UK, for couples from various walks of life. In this article, family lawyers Zoë Bloom and Hilary Pennington-Mellor, along with tax and wealth management lawyer Sarah Noake, explain why prenuptial agreements can work for any couple.

What's mine is mine

As the age of those entering into first-time marriages continues to rise, it's logical to expect many of them to have spent time amassing more, in terms of assets, on their own, which they want to shield from the prospect of divorce. Nuptial agreements form the best insurance parties can enter into, to give certainty in the event of a family breakdown. The only possible argument for them being "not relevant" is in circumstances where there is only enough money available to meet the separating parties basic needs, in terms of where they will live and how they will be supported following a divorce. Even then, when coupled with mortgage capacity and the expectation that parties move to cheaper parts of town, or perhaps rent, a prenuptial agreement will help determine the best outcome for the parties with limited court interference.

Nuptial agreements are usually entered into when times are good and there is a common intention to find an agreement which works best for both parties. That is a far better environment from which to come to an agreement which has the potential to work in the long term and be fair. Negotiating agreements after the end of a relationship, when parties are filled with animosity, distrust and bruised emotions cannot be a good time to find workable solutions for the common good.

In the courtroom

While these agreements are not legally valid, their terms need to be transposed into a consent order at the point of divorce and they always carry the risk of causing disagreements – if the court is asked to rule on the outcome, the strong likelihood is that, in the absence of vitiating circumstances (e.g. one party was forced to sign or they did not have the opportunity to seek legal advice), then the court will do its best to stick to the terms of the agreement. It will usually come away from the terms only if they are very unfair or unworkable and even then, will often stick as closely to the agreement as it can. Many judges take the view that if there was an agreement and one party acted in a particular way because they thought there was an agreement that agreement should hold, if possible.

Zoë Bloom says "I was recently in court with a client who told me she had approached a solicitor to ask whether she should enter a nuptial agreement to ring fence her £134,000 contribution to the purchase price of the family home and was told not to bother. I am told that she was advised that, in circumstances like hers, it was a pointless exercise and the court would override the agreement in the interests of achieving fairness between her and her ex-husband. Apparently, that solicitor had equated fairness with equality and determined that the court would simply divide the property in half regardless of any agreements which had been entered into. Thus far, the client had spent £20,000 trying to secure her contribution of £134,000. In the alternative, a nuptial agreement would have cost £3–5,000 + VAT for advice for both parties and would have hopefully saved the £20,000 court costs. I am increasingly arranging to meet parties together with the other legal advisor to thrash out an agreement in a morning. Everyone leaves the meeting with a full copy of a signed and agreed nuptial agreement. This saves hours of time in sending copies between legal advisors, amending drafts and negotiating terms. It gives the parties a far better sense of control over the process and input into their wishes and avoids everything being dragged out which can lead to disagreements."

Consider the circumstances

Hilary Pennington-Mellor adds "All those contemplating marriage will be wise to consider the financial consequences of marriage and of marital breakdown. Think of the consequences to others where there is a family business, partnership or shareholding, where there are existing dependents, if one party introduces significant assets, or if there is inherited wealth, or significant disparity of asset base. If one intended spouse has assets or resources overseas (for example the US) both may need advice on otherwise unforeseen taxation consequences of property ownership and worldwide income. Also consider jurisdictional points, and laws regulating marriage divorce and child rearing in another country. There is still no absolutely watertight route to limit or define the assets receivable by one party to marriage on separation following marital breakdown. Judges are increasingly willing to grant a degree of autonomy to separating couples to allow them to decide how they will divide assets on divorce, but the court retains power to make an order which does not reflect the parties agreement in its entirety. But the court will have regard to a properly made pre-marital agreement and it is likely to be influential although not enforceable."

How do prenups work overseas?

"Pre-nuptial agreements are often part of an estate plan (wills, documents covering loss of capacity, setting up trusts) that clients undertake, particularly in civil code countries or America, says Sarah Noake.

"It can be a challenge for clients, who become UK residents, as they may not realise that the English courts take a different view of pre-nuptial agreements than their home country. It is important for couples who have moved to the UK from abroad, and end up divorcing in the UK to take advice to try and ensure that the settlement they receive is dealt with as tax efficiently as possible, particularly if they remain UK resident. For example, they may wish to seek advice on their existing planning arrangements, which most likely would need updating, as well as seeking advice on the tax efficiency of their arrangements."

Prenups may form part of an estate plan but it's important to remember that they are not a substitute for one. They cannot be used as an alternative for a will and, even if a couple has entered into a prenuptial agreement, each partner should ensure that they still invest in a legally binding will in order to protect their personal wealth.

Choosing to take out a prenuptial agreement doesn't need to be costly in both time and money. With the right guidance, it can serve as an all-important sense of financial security, for all parties involved.

14 April 2016

⇨ The above information is reprinted with kind permission from Keystone Law. Please visit www. keystonelaw.co.uk for further information.

Common-law marriage

Understanding the myth of common-law marriage.

Contrary to popular belief, there is no such thing as a 'common-law marriage'. In England and Wales only people who are married, whether of the same sex or not, or those in civil partnerships can rely on the laws about dividing up finances when they divorce or dissolve their marriage.

The assumption by many unmarried couples in a long-standing relationship that they have acquired rights similar to those of married couples is wrong. This common misconception needs to be addressed, particularly as for many years official statistics show numbers of marriages in decline as more people choose to cohabit (living together without being married).

Many people also believe that by having a child together they acquire legal rights, whether married, in a civil partnership, or not. This is also not true. Although there is scope to apply to court for financial provision when there are children, such orders are made for the benefit of the child and only couples who are married or in a civil partnership acquire legal rights and responsibilities in relation to each other.

Your rights if you split up

For couples who are not married or in a civil partnership, if you split up your partner would not (except in certain types of cases) have to pay you maintenance even if you stayed at home to look after your children – but they would still have to pay child maintenance.

For couples who rented together, if you were not named on the rental agreement you will have no automatic right to stay if they walk out or ask you to leave and you would be left to apply to court for an order giving the right to occupy, the outcome of which is uncertain. If your ex-partner owned your home, and there is no other agreement in place, you have no right to stay if they ask you to leave.

Similarly, if you are not married or in a civil partnership, any savings or possessions your ex acquired out of their own money will not be shared with you although lump sum orders can be made in certain circumstances in proceedings where there are children.

To protect yourself if anything happens, you could consider entering into a contract with your partner to decide how money and property should be divided if you separate. These are known as 'Cohabitation Contracts' or 'agreements' and can be drafted by a solicitor.

If your partner dies

If your partner dies and you were not married or in a civil partnership, and they haven't made a will, you have no automatic entitlement to inherit anything from them, including your family home, even if it's in their name or if you own it jointly as 'tenants in common'. You would be left to make an application to court for provision from the estate as a dependent; these applications are uncertain and costly.

You are also not entitled to any state bereavement benefit or a state pension based on a percentage of your ex's national insurance contributions, even if you stayed at home to care for children and depended on your partner's income.

Rights for cohabiting couples in Scotland

The issue of unmarried couples misunderstanding their rights has already created a divide in the UK as since 2006 those who cohabit in Scotland have certain protections. The Scottish Parliament took the step to update Scottish law to reflect the way families choose to live and to ensure that any rights that already existed for cohabiting couples but were restricted to opposite sex couples only should be extended to include same-sex couples. The 2006 Act also provides a set of basic rights for cohabitants in Scotland whose relationship ends covering:

⇨ the sharing of household goods, bought during the time the couple lived together. This means that if you cannot agree about who owns any household goods, the law will assume that you both own it jointly and must share it or share what it is worth;

⇨ an equal share in money derived from an allowance made by one or other of the couple for household expenses and/or any property bought out of that money. It is important to understand that this does not apply to the house that the couple live in;

⇨ financial provision when, as a result of the decisions the couple made together during the relationship, one partner has been financially disadvantaged. This means, for example, if the couple

decided that one partner would give up a career to look after their children, they can ask the court to look at the effect that decision had on that partner's ability to earn money after the relationship has ended;

⇨ an assumption that both parents will continue to share the cost of childcare if they had children together; and

⇨ a right to apply to the court for an award from the estate (property) if their partner dies without leaving a will. Before this, if a cohabiting partner died without leaving a will the surviving partner was not entitled to anything from the deceased partner's estate. Sometimes this meant that they

had to move out of the house they had lived in together. The surviving partner will now be able to ask the court to consider giving them something from the estate. If the deceased partner was still married at the time of death, the spouse will still be legally entitled to a share of the estate.

This article was contributed to by Richard Busby, Family Law solicitor and Partner, Fisher Meredith.

⇨ The above information is reprinted with kind permission from Family Lives. Please visit www.familylives. org.uk for further information.

Common-law marriage myth highlights desperate need for reform

An article from The Conversation.

THE CONVERSATION

By Helen Jenks, Associate Professor, The University of Law

Your common-law wife and husband do not exist.

Next month will see the latest stage in the latest attempt to improve the legal standing for people that live together but choose not to marry. With nearly six million unmarried couples living outside marriage or a civil partnership in the UK, there is a real urgency for legal clarity for cohabitants who find themselves separating.

Not least, because of the persistence of the so called "common-law marriage myth" where assumptions still remain that if you live with a partner for a set amount of time you automatically gain a right to certain financial remedies in the event of separation. This is simply not the case.

In February 2013, the charity OnePlusOne found that 47% of UK citizens aged between 18 and 34 mistakenly assumed that cohabiting couples have the same legal rights as their married counterparts. This was a dismal improvement from the British Social Attitudes survey in 2008 which found that 51% of respondents believed

that the common-law marriage myth was real, despite campaigns to dispel the misunderstanding.

It's no surprise then, that lawyers are painfully familiar with people referring to their common-law wife or husband when in fact this doesn't exist in any legal sense.

Although couples can use cohabitation contracts to set out their legal position, few couples actually take advantage of them due to the lack of knowledge about their rights. And if they do have to rely on a contract in the event of the relationship breaking down, then the court can only deal with it the way it would any other contract – which does not lend itself to resolving such family disputes. If cohabiting couples are to be treated fairly, then reform is needed to properly clarify their legal position.

A long, long road

Previous attempts at a fix have failed. In 2007 the Law Commission published a report calling for reform and in December 2008 Lord Lester introduced a Private Members' Bill

to address the issue. It failed to even pass the committee stage. In 2011 the Law Commission reiterated its call for reform after the Government published a statement announcing their intention not to take the matter further.

Practising barrister and peer, Jonathan Marks QC, is the latest contender seeking to bring about change in the rights of cohabitants, by introducing another Private Members' Bill to settle the issue. The Bill was read last October and is set to be reintroduced in June this year.

The Bill seeks to allow couples who live together (including those with children) and those who have lived together for a continuous period of two years or more to be able to seek similar rights to those that married couples are already awarded in the divorce courts. The Bill has the caveat that either individual applying must have suffered either an economic disadvantage, or their ex-partner has retained a benefit.

Cause for hope

So why should Lord Marks' Bill succeed where others have failed? Part of the problem has been the perception by many that strengthening cohabitant's rights is often perceived as undermining the traditional institution of marriage – an issue which reached a crescendo with the introduction of marriage for same-sex couples. Now that same-sex couples can marry, it appears there is a real scope for change.

The pace of reform has also been hampered from opposition from a proportion of cohabitants who prefer the situation where no legal rights accrue as a result of their relationship. Significantly, Lord Marks' Bill allows cohabitants to opt out of the legal protection being offered.

In 2013, the family lawyer's organisation, Resolution, found that 69% of MPs agree that a mistaken belief exists around common-law marriage among their constituents, while 57% also believed that the law needed to change to provide greater protection for unmarried couples on separation.

It seems like a happy confluence of events. Opinion in Westminster and the success of the Same-Sex Marriage Act could well translate into legal certainty for cohabitants, who at the moment remain in legal limbo in the event of separation.

28 August 2014

⇨ The above information is reprinted with kind permission from *The Conversation*. Please visit www.theconversation.com for further information.

UK cohabitees have greater financial risk, as confusion reigns over legal and benefit entitlements

⇨ Half (51%) of cohabitees think government benefits are biased in favour of married couples

⇨ But confusion persists among cohabitees around their legal entitlements: nearly one in five (19%) wrongly believe they are eligible for bereavement benefit

⇨ Over a third (36%) do not know that the Marriage Allowance exists

⇨ A third (33%) of cohabitees have not yet named the beneficiary of their pension

⇨ Cohabitees' finances are in poorer health than married couples, with lower incomes and less savings

⇨ Three quarters (74%) of cohabitees do not have a will and 64% have no life insurance

⇨ One in ten (10%) cohabitees also admit to only being with their partner as they cannot afford to separate

Nearly two million UK cohabitees (51%) say government policies are weighted in favour of married couples, but many are still confused about the financial risks they are running, Aviva's *Family Finances* research shows.

Measures such as the Marriage Allowance and Inheritance and Capital Gains Tax breaks are perceived by 1.7 million cohabitees to leave them on an unequal footing – with only 12% disagreeing with the view that policy favours those who marry.

But in a sign of how unprepared cohabiting couples are if the worst were to happen, nearly one in five (19% or 627,000) think they are entitled to bereavement benefit or allowances if their partner dies, despite the fact upcoming legislation will reaffirm that this does not apply to cohabitees. With over a third (38%) of cohabiting couples also having dependent children[1], and 74% (or 2.4 million couples) not having a Will, such confusion could add to the financial stress in the event of a parent's death.

The research highlights how cohabitees are already less likely to feel financially secure (68%) than married couples (76%) and are often in poorer financial health, as well as having significantly less financial protection in place.

The findings are significant as the number of cohabitees has soared to 3.3 million, more than doubling since 1996 and accounting for 17% of all families compared to 9% 20 years ago.[2] In contrast, while married couples still represent the largest family group (12.6 million), their share has dropped from 76% in 1996 to 67% today.

Though the Cohabitation Rights Bill is currently progressing in Parliament[3], which will give cohabitees certain protections, the Bill is not expected to be finalised any time soon. As this family type continues to grow, it is vital cohabitees are helped to understand the financial implications of their relationship choices.

When it comes to tax rights and obligations, nearly one in five (18% or 594,000 couples) think they are eligible for the same Capital Gains Tax breaks as married couples, and 15% of cohabitees (495,000 couples) wrongly

1 ONS, *Families and Households in UK*, Nov 16

2 ONS, *Families and Households in UK*, Nov 16

3 Cohabitation Rights Bill, parliament.uk

believe they can pass on their assets to a surviving spouse without incurring any Inheritance Tax.

Over a third (36%) of cohabitees who intend to marry do not know that the Marriage Allowance actually exists.

Automatic pension rights?

More than one in five (21%) cohabitees believe they would inherit their partner's final salary pension if they passed away. However, not all schemes will pay benefits to unmarried partners in the event of death and it is important for long-term cohabitees to review their pension scheme rules. For schemes where unmarried partners are permitted to be beneficiaries, they need to be named as such on the nomination form; however, a third (33%) of cohabitees have not yet named the beneficiaries of their pension if they die and 6% don't know whether they have.

Financial vulnerabilities

Cohabitees' misunderstandings and sense of being disadvantaged are further compounded by the fact they tend to be in poorer overall financial health than married couples to begin with, and are less likely to have financial protection in place – putting them on a less-secure financial footing.

Aviva's data illustrates that cohabitees' monthly incomes are 14% lower compared to married people (£1,944 vs £2,265). This is partly due to age as 84% of 18–24s are cohabitees, compared to over half (54%) of 25–35s. That said, over a third (37%) of 36–45s and almost two fifths (39%) of 46–55s are cohabitees, highlighting that since cohabitating is a lifelong choice for some, financial weakness is not reserved to one generation.

Home-ownership levels are also significantly lower among cohabitees: 58% own their home outright or with a mortgage, compared to three quarters (74%) of married people – cohabitees are therefore less likely to have experienced a key trigger for taking out financial protection.

Three quarters of cohabitees (74%) do not have a will versus 61% of married couples, while almost two thirds (64%) of cohabitees do not have life

insurance compared with less than half (45%) of those who are married.

Only a minority of cohabitees (4%) have a precautionary arrangement, such as a cohabitation agreement, in place to protect their finances should a relationship break down. Typically the modest cost of such an agreement is around £300 – the same as organising a will.

Perceptions of affordability are a significant barrier for cohabitees when it comes to financial protection, and they are more likely than married people to have not even thought about taking out any financial cover for their loved ones or families.

Despite sharing a home, almost a third (31%) keep their money completely separate from their partner, nearly twice the proportion of married people that do the same (17%). One in ten (10%) cohabitees also admit to only being with their partner because they cannot afford to separate: equivalent to 330,000 couples across the UK.

Paul Brencher, Managing Director, Individual Protection, Aviva UK commented:

"Many couples in the UK are choosing to marry later or not at all. But

cohabitees do not enjoy the same financial benefits as those who are married or in a civil partnership.

"What is particularly concerning is the extent to which some cohabitees falsely believe they are entitled to the same benefits as those who are married. Such confusion has the potential to cause significant financial stress should their family experience an unexpected change in circumstance.

"Though it is welcome that more rights are on the horizon through the Cohabitation Rights Bill, cohabiting couples should take the time now to better understand their financial situation in order to plan effectively for the future. We must strive to create a mind-set among all UK family types that proactively planning for the long term is important not just for those who are married but for all those who want to enjoy a comfortable future without the fear of financial uncertainty."

15 February 2017

⇨ The above information is reprinted with kind permission from Aviva. Please visit www.aviva.com for further information.

How to Make a Living Together Agreement

If you are moving in or living with your partner and aren't married, it is a really good idea to make a Living Together Agreement. This explains why having a Living Together Agreement is a brilliant way to protect yourself and your partner, and takes you step-by-step through the process.

What is a Living Together Agreement?

A Living Together Agreement (or Cohabitation Agreement as it is sometimes called) is simply a record of what you have agreed about how you will own and share things. It encourages you to think about easy and fair ways to organise your day-to-day finances and ensures that if your relationship ended, neither of you would lose out financially – unless that is what you had agreed. All couples who live together would benefit from making one.

An agreement that sets out what would happen if you did split up isn't an admission that you think you will, any more than taking out building insurance means that you think your house will fall down. In fact, it can strengthen your relationship by helping both partners to feel happier and more secure.

Joe's story

"When we bought a flat together my girlfriend suggested I paid the mortgage and she paid all the other bills (which added up to the same). We'd been doing that for a year when my mum mentioned she thought that would mean I had more right to the flat than my girlfriend. We both knew that wasn't fair, so when I suggested making a Living Together Agreement she agreed straight away."

Why should we bother?

A Living Together Agreement helps you to discuss and agree how you will pay for things like the rent or mortgage, and household bills. In doing so, it can help you avoid the kind of arguments and minor worries that can build up over time.

But when it really comes in useful, is if you split up. Unfortunately, some couples do split up. Couples that live together have few rights or protections if it does all go wrong, no matter how committed to each other they were, or how long they have been together. (If you have children together, there are some things the law can help with, but not many.) Instead, couples have to try and work out how to divide their property, money and belongings on their own – when they are usually heartbroken or angry and not feeling terribly fair.

Couples who haven't made a Living Together Agreement often find that they have very different expectations of what should happen or ideas of what is fair. For couples who have been together a long time, it's hard to even remember who contributed what, let alone what you said about it at the time.

As unlikely as it seems, making a Living Together Agreement is actually a loving thing to do. It protects both yourself and your partner from unfairness and unpleasantness in the future, just in case.

Sandra's story

"We had lived together for seven years when things fell apart. I moved out and stayed with friends. I suddenly had no home, but what was even harder was not having anything! Everything stayed in the flat with Adam and I was so emotional, the last thing I wanted to do was go round and start trying to negotiate or take legal action. It all took months and eventually I ran out of energy. He ended up keeping everything basically. He was supposed to buy me out of the house, but I ended up settling for a lot less than half. He wasn't trying to be unfair, it was just the circumstances. As long as I had to keep going back I couldn't move on."

When to make a Living Together Agreement

Ideally you would make a Living Together Agreement when you first move in together, but late is better than never, so even if you've already been together for 15 years it's still a good idea.

"My partner and I made a Living Together Agreement two or three years after we'd bought our flat together. Good job we did. Until we made the agreement we hadn't noticed that we had very different understandings of what we had agreed about the flat. I thought we owned it 50/50, but she thought she owned 65% of it because we had borrowed some money from her mum, even though we paid her back."

Is a Living Together Agreement legally binding?

Living Together Agreements have a slightly odd status in law. They aren't binding unless you write them as a formal legal deed, but the court will usually follow them as long as what you agreed is fair, and you were both honest about your finances when you made the agreement. A court is even more likely to uphold the agreement if both of you also had some legal advice about what you were doing before signing the agreement.

If you want to ensure it is binding, take your completed agreement to a solicitor and ask them to write it as a legal 'deed'.

Don't put it off

Hopefully you have decided you really should make a Living Together Agreement – please don't put it off. Like making a will, it doesn't seem urgent and so too many people never get round to it. We're sure you can think of more fun things to do with your evening – but this is probably the most useful thing you can do.

How I suggested it to my partner...

We asked readers who had made a Living Together Agreement to tell us how they first suggested it to their partner.

"Tash has always been clear that she never ever wanted to get married. So when she got pregnant with our eldest, I went down on one knee and proposed a living together agreement." Aidan

"I just told him I hope our relationship lasts forever, but just in case it doesn't we should make a living together agreement. If the worst does happen and we do split up, I don't want us to hate each other." Neelam

"I'd heard about Living Together Agreements and mentioned it to my partner one night. I said I didn't think we needed to because, if we did split up, I thought we'd be really fair about money and the flat we rent. She said that actually, she didn't think she would be and as she is better at arguing than me, we should probably make an agreement now. The next day she had printed off the forms and we filled them in. Not the funnest evening we've ever had but definitely pleased we have it in the drawer, just in case." Suzi

"I earn more than my partner, always have. When I first mentioned Living Together Agreements to her, it didn't go well. I'm not sure if she got it confused with a celebrity pre-nup or what, but she definitely thought it was about me protecting what is mine. It was only when we were discussing what we would put in it that she realised that wasn't it." Tom

⇨ The above information is reprinted with kind permission from Advicenow. Please visit www.advicenow.org.uk for further information.

Forced marriage

Because forced marriage is illegal, it can happen in secret and can also be planned by parents, family or religious leaders. It may involve physical abuse, sexual abuse or emotional abuse.

Being forced to marry

Nobody has the right to force you to do something you don't want to do. You can talk to a counsellor any time about how you feel and if you're having problems with your family.

Some families force their children to marry because they:

⇨ think it's an important part of religion or culture

⇨ are worried about the family's reputation and honour (in some cultures also known as 'izzat')

⇨ want all of the family's money to stay together

⇨ want to marry their children off in exchange for money

⇨ don't approve of their child being gay, lesbian, bisexual or transgender

⇨ don't want their children to have relationships or sex

⇨ feel pressured by the community or other family members to follow traditions

⇨ want to keep family values and honour.

But none of these reasons are okay. And nobody has the right to force you into marriage.

What to do if you're being forced into marriage

Remember that if you're being forced into marrying someone you don't want to, this is wrong and it's also against the law. It can feel like you have no control, but it's important to think about your future, your safety and what a forced marriage would be like for you.

It's possible that your parents or family would force you to marry because they think it's the best thing for you. This doesn't make things okay and you can get help to stop this from happening.

You might love your parents but might also feel unsure about why you're being forced to marry. You might be told that you're bringing shame on your family if you don't marry. Your parents might even say that they'll disown you. This is emotional abuse.

If you can't talk to your parents, maybe you can think of another adult who you trust, like a family member, teacher or school nurse. It's important to let someone know as quickly as possible so that you can be safe and get help.

Your rights

Forced marriages happen in many religions and nationalities, and can affect both boys and girls. It doesn't only happen to young people, it can happen to adults too. There are some people and communities that think forced marriage is okay.

But it's important to remember that all major religions (Muslim, Hindu, Sikh, Christian and Jewish) are against forced marriage. Forced marriage is never okay, and it's important to remember there is help available.

Forced marriage is against the law in the UK and you have a right to say no if you're being made to marry someone who you don't want to. The minimum age for marriage in the UK is 16.

You have the right to:

⇨ choose who you marry, when you marry or whether you want to get married or not

⇨ make decisions and to be able to tell someone about what's happening to you

⇨ feel safe and to ask for help

⇨ say no and explain that you don't feel happy with what is happening.

You might worry that if you tell someone then your parents or other people could get into trouble. Or you may think it will make things worse. You don't have to deal with this on your own. There are people who won't judge you and who will support you

with what you're going through. You can contact a counsellor in private at any time and talk about anything.

If you're being taken to another country to get married

If your parents or someone else is taking you to another country to force you to get married, this is wrong. It is also breaking the law. But you can get help.

If you know you are going to be taken out of the country you can contact Childline or the Forced Marriage Unit and explain what is happening.

⇨ Get a Forced Marriage Protection Order. The Forced Marriage Unit can help you get this. It's a legal document that can stop you being taken abroad and forced into marriage. It can also help bring you back to the UK if you are taken out of the country. If a court makes an order for you, they will protect you from anyone trying to force you into marriage.

⇨ Speak to security staff at the airport if you're already at the airport or travelling. You can speak to airport police officers, or call 999 for urgent help.

⇨ Think very carefully before you leave the country. It could be much harder to get help when you are abroad.

⇨ Tell someone you trust. Try to let a trusted adult or close friend know that you're being taken away and keep their contact details with you.

⇨ Think of a code word that will let someone you trust know you're in danger that only you and they know.

⇨ Take information with you like contact details for the Forced Marriage Unit or British Embassy in the country you are visiting in case you need help.

If you're already abroad

You might think you're going on a family holiday but then realise that plans have been made for you to get married. In some cultures, families might plan a holiday around the time of religious festivals.

It can be very scary if you are already abroad and then realise what is happening. You could contact someone who you trust in the UK who could tell your teacher or let the police know. They can tell the Forced Marriage Unit who could help you

return. You could also contact the British Embassy in the country where you are – they can get help for you to leave the country and stay safe.

If you worry your parents will disown you if you don't

If your parents have threatened to harm you or to disown you if you don't go ahead with a forced marriage, you can get help. You don't have to cope on your own. There are organisations like the Karma Nirvana and Freedom Charity that support young people who have nowhere to go. They can work with social services to get you help with finding a place to stay.

Childline is a safe place to talk and the counsellors can help you find the support you need.

Is it different to an arranged marriage?

A forced marriage is different from an arranged marriage.

Arranged marriage:

⇨ is a cultural tradition

⇨ you have a choice.

Forced marriage:

⇨ is an abuse of human rights

⇨ you don't have a choice.

Sometimes an arranged marriage can lead to a forced marriage. For example, if you agree to marry someone but then change your mind and decide not to.

If your parents or family don't accept your decision and still make you go ahead with the marriage, this becomes a forced marriage.

If you need support and someone to talk to, you can and speak to one of our counsellors. It's free to call and confidential.

⇨ The above information is reprinted with kind permission from Childline. Please visit www.childline.org.uk for further information.

© Childline 2017

Criminalising forced marriage has not helped its victims

THE CONVERSATION

An article from The Conversation.

By Aisha K. Gill, Associate Professor in Criminology, University of Roehampton

In the year since forced marriage was criminalised in the UK, only one conviction has taken place. In June, a 34-year-old man was jailed for forcing a 25-year-old woman to marry him under duress. Merthyr Crown Court in Wales heard that the man – who was already married to someone else – repeatedly raped his victim over a period of months, threatened to publish footage of her having a shower and told her that her parents would be killed, unless she agreed to become his wife.

The defendant was put on the sex offenders' register and sentenced to 16 years in custody, to be released under an extended licence for another five years afterwards. This is an important case, which will raise questions about whether these offences – which also included rape, voyeurism and bigamy, alongside forced marriage – could have been prosecuted under the existing criminal law.

Before forced marriage was criminalised, the Forced Marriage (Civil Protection) Act 2007 enabled courts to issue protection orders against those who attempt or conspire to force someone into marriage. Between November 2008 (when the Act came into force) and September 2014, there were 762 applications filed for forced marriage protection orders. During this same period, 785 forced marriage protection orders were issued (some of which may have been interim orders, issued during other proceedings).

Last year, the Government's Forced Marriage Unit provided support and assistance for 1,267 possible cases of forced marriage. It is troubling, then, that there has been only one conviction since June last year under the 2014 Act.

An adversarial system

Laws are only effective when properly enforced. Those who believe the new sanctions will eradicate forced marriage overlook the fact that criminal prosecutions require a high standard of proof. This standard will have a dramatic effect on the rate of successful prosecutions.

Failed prosecutions, and cases that do not proceed to prosecution may result in victims being discredited or shamed within their family and community, while those at fault may feel exonerated. This raises the risk that victims will suffer isolation and further abuse, because their family and community are likely to ostracise them, or even seek revenge.

The adversarial British criminal justice system requires that victims and witnesses give evidence in court, and submit to being cross-examined. The rules of the court require that the prosecution must disclose all their evidence to the defence. This includes highly sensitive information gathered by the police, local authorities and other organisations when a complaint is made by a victim or information provided by a third party about a forced marriage.

If the case proceeds to court, the victim and any witnesses may, in some cases, face the sharing and discussion of this information in public. Apart from placing them at risk of harm, the impact of being made to participate in difficult, and often lengthy, public proceedings is likely to be significant. These practicalities demand further reflection from those who make the law.

Access to justice

Even if prosecution is successful, victims may still endure other challenges, and require extensive support from different services. For one thing, it's often the case that the victims of forced marriage, and those at risk, need assistance from specialist support services, in order to access justice in the first place.

Research by Rights of Women reveals that many victims of forced marriage cannot afford to pay for the legal assistance they require. For instance, foreign nationals may require immigration advice and assistance, while British citizens may need advice regarding family law remedies like marriage annulments, or contact with their children.

Cuts to Legal Aid have had a negative impact on victims' ability to obtain vital legal advice. As forced marriage cases are often extremely complex in a legal sense, it is crucial that advice is freely available to enable those in need to seek justice. And legal remedies are only one aspect of addressing forced marriage.

Legislation fails to address the day-to-day issues associated with protecting and supporting victims, and there have been no additional resources announced to meet these needs. This places the responsibility for supporting victims onto charities – particularly women's charities, since the vast majority of cases involve female victims.

The need for support

Rashida Manjoo – the UN's Special Rapporteur on violence against women – has called for the UK Government to "urgently evaluate the way women's support services are funded and then act to ensure a network of women-centred services are available to all who need them". In her report on violence against women in the UK, its causes and consequences – presented at the United Nations on 17 June 2015 – Manjoo points out that funding for these charities often falls short.

Evidence demonstrates that actual and potential victims of forced marriage are far more likely to approach and trust specialist black and minority ethnic women's services, rather than the state agencies. Yet few of these services currently receive adequate funding. And the limited resources available to local authorities often means that appropriate accommodation is all but non-existent. It is vital that these services are properly funded, even in times of austerity.

The situation is even more urgent for the 11% of victims who are under 16 years of age: they have little recourse to services, apart from overstretched and cash-strapped local authorities, many of whom are already overburdened with cases of child abuse and unable to provide appropriate accommodation.

The national shortage of suitable foster homes, and the lack of specialist carers with appropriate training in cultural sensitivity adds to the challenges faced by victims of forced marriage. This kind of training is urgently needed to ensure that criminal and civil support systems – including child protection services – are working effectively.

Ultimately, the success of the stand-alone law on forced marriage will depend on how effective it proves for victims. At present, too little consideration has been paid to the practicalities of this legislation, and its effect on victims themselves.

17 July 2015

⇨ The above information is reprinted with kind permission from *The Conversation*. Please visit www.theconversation.com for further information.

CHILD MARRIAGE IS ANY FORMAL MARRIAGE OR INFORMAL UNION WHERE ONE OR BOTH OF THE PARTIES ARE UNDER 18 YEARS OF AGE.

EACH YEAR, 15 MILLION GIRLS ARE MARRIED BEFORE THE AGE OF 18. THAT IS 28 GIRLS EVERY MINUTE... ONE EVERY TWO SECONDS.

Child marriage happens across countries, cultures and religions.

Child marriage violates girls' rights to health, education and opportunity. It exposes girls to violence throughout their lives, and traps them in a cycle of poverty.

If there is no reduction in child marriage, the global number of women married as children will reach 1.2 billion by 2050, with devastating consequences for the whole world.

700 MILLION WOMEN
More than 700 million women, and over 150 million men, already suffer the consequences of child marriage.

Child marriage looks different from one community to the next. Solutions must be local and contextual.

Source: Girls Not Brides 2017 www.girlsnotbrides.org

The haven for honeymooners where everyone gets divorced

By Oliver Smith

Brad Pitt and Angelina Jolie's sudden split may well have shocked the Western world, but given how commonplace divorce has become– particularly in the United States – perhaps it shouldn't have.

The US has the sixth highest divorce rate of any country, with 3.6 annual divorces per 1,000 inhabitants, according to the most recent figures available. But America has some way to go to match the divorce capital of the world. Ironically, given that it's so popular with honeymooners, it is the Maldives. The island nation has a divorce rate of 10.97, earning it recognition in the *Guinness Book of Records*. The UN even estimates that the average Maldivian woman, by the age of 30, has been divorced three times.

Why is the rate so high in the Maldives? Various reasons have been cited. Perhaps the most compelling is that, as in other Muslim societies, where premarital sex is taboo, many marry young, but, under the country's mixed Sharia and common law system, they can then secure a divorce relatively easily when things don't work out. Others have blamed a lack of childcare facilities combined with a rise in women entering the workforce.

Russia, Belarus, Latvia and another tropical idyll – Aruba – fill the gaps in between the US and the Maldives. The UK divorce rate is two, putting it tied for 38th of the 104 destinations to feature. The lowest divorce rates are often found in countries with large Catholic populations, such as Chile, Colombia and Ireland, as well as Muslim countries like Libya, Uzbekistan and Bahrain.

The 20 places where divorce is most common

1. Maldives – 10.97 per year per 1,000 inhabitants
2. Russia – 4.5
3. Aruba – 4.4
4. Belarus – 4.1
5. Latvia – 3.6
6. United States – 3.6
7. Lithuania – 3.5
8. Gibraltar – 3
9. Moldova – 3
10. Belgium – 3
11. Cuba – 2.9
12. Switzerland – 2.8
13. Ukraine – 2.8
14. Denmark – 2.8
15. Hong Kong – 2.76
16. Jordan – 2.6
17. Czech Republic – 2.5
18. Portugal – 2.5
19. Costa Rica – 2.5
20. Sweden – 2.5

20 September 2016

⇨ The above information is reprinted with kind permission from *The Telegraph*. Please visit www.telegraph.co.uk for further information.

British families among most unstable in the developed world

Britain has some of the most unstable families in the developed world, a new study has found.

Figures released by the Marriage Foundation show that the majority of British children born to co-habiting couples will see their parents break up, while a third of British 12-year-olds have seen their married parents separate.

The Foundation's Chairman, Sir Paul Coleridge, described the figures as a "loud wake-up call" to the UK's family breakdown "epidemic".

Britain has highest breakdown rate

The international study of 100 countries found that three in five British children (62%) born to unmarried couples experience family breakdown before they hit their teen years. This stood in contrast to 45% of American children, 15% of Belgian children and 6% of Spanish children.

But even married families in Britain were found to have one of the highest rates of family breakdown in Europe.

A third of British 12-year-olds whose parents were married when they were born have experienced family breakdown – compared to 9% in Austria and 11% in France.

Marriage correlates with stability

More generally, the study showed that across the globe, cohabiting couples are more likely to be unstable than those who are married.

In the UK, children born to cohabiting parents are 94% more likely to see their parents break up before they reach the age of 12, than children who are born to married parents.

Spain, Bulgaria, Italy and Georgia had the best records of families staying together.

The study's conclusion states: "Using both individual-level and country-level data, we have shown that births to cohabiting unions contribute to instability in children's family lives."

"There is much variation between countries in the amount of instability, but there are few exceptions to the pattern: children born to marital unions have the best chance of stability across various cultures, legal systems, welfare regimes and levels of cohabitation."

Marriage, not education, is key

The study also found that higher levels of education do not correlate with couples staying together.

In the overwhelming majority of countries, the least educated married couples were shown to be far less likely to break up than the most educated cohabiting parents.

The conclusion went on: "While growth in cohabitation tends to close the socioeconomic gap between cohabiting and married couples, it does not close the stability gap for their children. In other words, marriage seems to be associated with more family stability for children across much of the globe."

"Is anyone listening to the children?"

Sir Paul Coleridge commented:

"The findings of this study are yet another loud wake-up call about the lack of regard we have in the UK towards the vital importance of family stability. How many more surveys and reports do we need before government puts this problem at the very top of the social justice agenda?

"No doubt our all-consuming obsession with personal development, self-reliance and career aspiration

benefits the economy, but is anyone listening to the children or feeling their pain?"

Championing marriage

He went on: "This research is yet further justification for continuing to champion marriage over all other arrangements leading to the birth and upbringing of children. Across the globe the children of married couples fare best.

"Stability is the name of the game; stability in a child's life is the number one key factor over all others.

"We are facing a family breakdown epidemic in this country, the highest rates of family collapse on record ever."

9 February 2017

⇨ The above information is reprinted with kind permission from Christian Concern. Please visit www.christianconcern.com for further information.

Does religion help couples stay together?

I'm often asked if Christians have lower divorce rates than anyone else. Although I point out that I don't know of any UK studies on this, evidence from the US is fairly mixed that religion – or 'religiosity' as it's usually called in the academic papers – is linked to higher rates of stability.

In any case, if you were going to make a social science hypothesis based on what you read in the Bible, there's a much better candidate than simply whether one subscribes to a certain religion or not. Jesus is reported in the gospels as saying: "What God has joined together, let man not separate." Therefore anyone who includes God in their marriage ought to do better.

And so it seems. US studies show very nicely that people who apply their faith into their marriage – those who see their marriage as 'God-inspired' or 'sacred' – tend to do better.

Anyway, I thought it was about time we had a look at the link between religion and stability. So I asked my long-time colleague, and world-class stats expert, Professor Steve McKay at the University of Lincoln, if we could do a study on this.

Using data from the Millennium Cohort Study, we looked at the religious and ethnic groupings of 10,000 or so new mothers who had babies in the years 2000 or 2001, and then followed them through to when their children were 11 years old to see who was still together and who wasn't.

You can read our full report online, published in 2016 and reported in the *Daily Telegraph*.

Our initial finding was that Christian and Muslim mothers overall were more likely to stay together than non-religious mothers. The same was true for Christian fathers, though not Muslim fathers.

However, we also looked at a whole load of other background factors and their independent influence on stability. As we had already found in some of our other research, being married, being older, being better educated, planning your pregnancy, and being happy in your relationship all have their own effect on a couple's odds of staying together.

But when we added these factors into the mix and compared like-with-like, the apparent advantage in stability to Christian mothers and fathers disappeared. The reason they tended to do better was down to their greater likelihood of being better educated and also being married.

So it's being married that is partly responsible for making Christian parents more likely to stay together, even if the fact that they are Christians makes them more likely to get married in the first place.

Yet even after taking all these background factors into account, and comparing people of similar age, education, marital status and relationship happiness, two groups stood out in terms of their religion or ethnicity.

Muslim mothers did especially well. Because we included relationship happiness in the mix, we can rule out any suspicion that they are somehow repressed as a group.

Black fathers did especially badly. Even if they were married and happy, they were still more likely to split up compared to other fathers.

Both of these findings suggest there is an important influence of culture – rather than religion – in play here. One effect is positive and one is negative. It leaves us asking questions about what they are doing differently, whether they think differently about marriage and relationships, and whether they have different levels of social support

What is it that makes Muslim mothers especially stable in their relationships, yet Muslim fathers are no different to anyone else?

What is it that makes black fathers especially unstable in their relationships, whereas this is not the case for black mothers?

November 2016

⇨ The above information is reprinted with kind permission from the Marriage Foundation. Please visit www.marriagefoundation.org.uk for further information.

Staying in an unhappy marriage "is for the best"

People who stick with their spouse through unhappy times are better off in the long run, the Marriage Foundation claims.

In new research, the campaign group insisted that "unhappiness in a marriage is often just a short-term and fixable problem".

Although the Foundation admitted that some parents are unhappy with their marriage following the birth of their first child, they claimed that the majority of those couples – seven out of every ten – stayed together and 68 per cent of them were happy ten years later. In fact, 27 per cent of those who were unsatisfied when they became parents had become "extremely happy" within a decade.

These figures were based on an analysis of 15,207 parents whose children were born in 2000 or 2001. This data was gathered as part of the Millennium Cohort Study conducted by the Centre for Longitudinal Studies, an economic research organisation based at the University of London.

Marriage Foundation research director Harry Benson said that despite popular belief "staying in an unhappy marriage could be the best thing you ever do". Most married couples experience moments of stress or strain at some point but "apart from the fortunately extremely rare cases where the relationship involves abuse, most couples can work through the difficulties to be happy later on" he claimed.

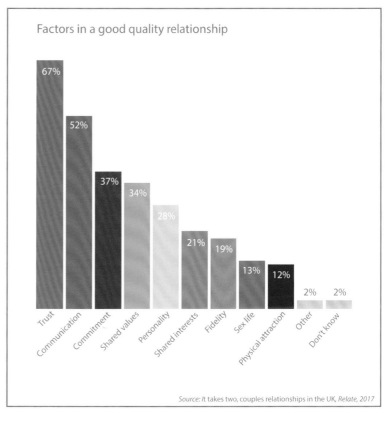

Factors in a good quality relationship

Factor	%
Trust	67%
Communication	52%
Commitment	37%
Shared values	34%
Personality	28%
Shared interests	21%
Fidelity	19%
Sex life	13%
Physical attraction	12%
Other	2%
Don't know	2%

Source: It takes two, couples relationships in the UK, Relate, 2017

Former High Court Judge Sir Paul Coleridge founded the Marriage Foundation in 2012. He said one of the biggest problems facing marriage was people's misconceptions about what goes into a relationship. He explained:

"They do not just happen. Just because each party is passionate about the other at the start does not automatically mean they will remain for ever at that high octane level without effort and without periods of unhappiness."

In 2015, a YouGov poll found that as many as 61 per cent of Britons have stayed in an unhappy relationship for much longer than they think they should have. Only six per cent of the more than 2,000 people surveyed claimed they had broken up with their partner soon after realising they were not a good match.

8 February 2017

⇨ The above information is reprinted with kind permission from Marilyn Stowe. Please visit http://www.marilynstowe.co.uk/2017/02/08/staying-unhappy-marriage-for-the-best/ for further information.

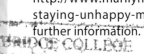

© Marilyn Stowe 2017

A guide to the divorce process in England and Wales

The divorce process in England and Wales has five separate steps, which can be completed without instructing a solicitor and spending over £1,000 on your divorce.

You will need to complete a D8 divorce petition, which is the main document in a divorce and then make two more separate applications to the court in order to complete the divorce procedure.

It is possible to complete the UK divorce process within three months – we've had clients complete within 12–14 weeks this year – but not everyone can expect their divorce process to be completed so quickly, with the average divorce case taking 18–20 weeks to finalise.

Steps to the divorce procedure in the UK

⇨ Find a valid ground for divorce to use

⇨ File a D8 divorce petition with the courts

⇨ Apply for a decree nisi

⇨ Apply for a decree absolute

Although there are only four steps necessary to obtain a divorce, there are parts of the divorce procedure where your spouse needs to acknowledge the divorce papers and respond to the court.

We have put together some detailed information on each step of the divorce procedure in England and Wales so that you understand exactly what is involved before you apply for a divorce.

The stages of the divorce process

Step 1 – file divorce petition

A divorce petition (D8) is filed at court setting out the ground for the divorce with the court fee of £550.00 (If applicable to you). The divorce petition is the main document in any divorce and is therefore essential that you complete this document correctly.

Step 2 – acknowlegement of service

The court will then send a copy of the divorce petition form to your spouse with an acknowledgement of service form to complete and return. If your spouse needs assistance in completing the form to make sure it's sent back to the courts correctly, they should look at a respondent in divorce service.

Step 3 – decree nisi

You can then apply for the Decree Nisi (the first decree), which is a document which states that the court cannot see a reason why you can't divorce.

Step 4 – decree nisi pronounced

The court will issue a certificate telling you when the decree nisi will be pronounced in court.

Step 5 – application for decree absolute

Six weeks after the decree nisi you can then apply to make the decree nisi, absolute (the final decree), which will end your marriage.

⇨ The above information is reprinted with kind permission from Divorce-Online. Please visit www. divorce-online.co.uk for further information.

2.87 million people across UK in distressed relationships

⇨ 2.87 million people (18% of married or cohabiting couples) are in distressed relationships*

⇨ This includes over 1.4 million families** at breaking point across the UK

⇨ Parents of under-16s are more likely to be in distressed relationships (22%)

⇨ Today, the charity Relate launches its first appeal to help address negative impacts of family breakdown and poor quality relationships

A staggering 2.87 million people across the UK are living in relationships which would be described within clinical practice as distressed, according a new study by Relate, the UK's leading relationships charity. This equates to 18% of married or cohabiting couples and 1.4 million UK families.

The charity is concerned that these poor quality relationships are having a detrimental impact on people's physical and mental health with many struggling to access the support they need and reaching breaking point. The figures are released as Relate launches its first national appeal, Breaking Point, calling for donations to help subsidise vital services to support families whose relationships and finances are under intense pressure.

The statistics are taken from Relate's report, *Relationship Distress Monitor*, which is published today (Wednesday 25 May) and is based on new analysis of data from the UK household longitudinal study, Understanding Society. The research, which had a sample size of 20,980, looked at key questions from a validated scale to measure relationship quality. These included how often couples argued, how frequently they considered separation or divorce, the extent of unhappiness in their relationship and how often they regretted being in their relationship.

The research also found that:

⇨ 9% of partners report at least occasionally*** considering divorce or separation

⇨ 10% of partners report at least occasionally regretting getting married or living together

⇨ 49% of partners report at least occasionally quarrelling – and 6.8% report severe levels

⇨ Parents of under-16s are more likely to be in distressed relationships – 22%.

A distressed relationship is one with a severe level of relationship problems, which has a clinically significant negative impact on partner's well being. Relate counsellor, Arabella Russell, said:

"Through my work I see countless couples in distressed relationships. Often the couples I see are arguing constantly with pressures such as jobs, finances and childcare putting their relationships under real strain. It's a very painful place to be and the impact it can have on the family is huge."

Surbiton mother of four, Julia Darbyshire, 47, attended Relate with her husband, Andy, 47, when their relationship reached breaking point. Julia said:

"We went to Relate when the pressures of work and childcare started to impact on our relationship. We were arguing a lot and our eldest son was noticing that we were at loggerheads. We had hit a real rocky patch but with the support of our counsellor, we were able to turn things around.

"Speaking to somebody objective was really helpful. Since attending the counselling sessions, things have really improved and we've gone on to have another two children together. We now feel we communicate more effectively and have the tools we need to address any issues that come up. I'd urge anyone to donate to Relate – I think it's so important that everyone can access support for their relationships, not just those who can afford it. Unhappy relationships can have a terrible effect on couples and their children but it doesn't have to be that way."

Relationship breakdown currently costs the UK economy £48billion a year. Relate highlights that as well as the economic cost, there is also a profound social and human cost of poor-quality relationships. Chris Sherwood, Chief Executive at Relate said:

"It is hugely concerning that 18% of UK married and cohabiting couples are in distressed relationships. Broken and unhealthy relationships can lead to debt, loneliness, health problems, depression, homelessness, criminality and can have a profound effect on children's life chances.

"Families can't go on like this. We need to make sure that Relate's services are available to everyone, not just those who can afford them, but we can't do so unless we get donations to subsidise the cost. That is why we are launching our Breaking Point appeal today, calling on people to donate to us to help families find the answer that's right for them, as with Relate's support a breaking point can become a turning point."

⇨ To donate to Relate, please www.relate.org.uk/donate

⇨ Read the report, Relationship Distress Monitor, (from Weds 25th May): http://bit.ly/23UGPLw

⇨ View the Breaking Point appeal video: https://www.youtube.com/watch?v=IHY-kh6c04c

Levels of relationship distress were estimated by analysing data from the Understanding Society survey. The most recent data were released November 2015, and the data were analysed over March-April 2016. The sample of people in relationships (married or cohabiting) was 20,980. Relationships were characterised as 'distressed' or 'non-distressed' by calculating respondents' answers to questions from a scientifically validated scale to measure relationship quality and the severity of relationship problems. For further information on the methodology, please see the research report.

** *We follow the ONS definition of 'families' in the Families and Households statistical bulletins: 'A family is a married, civil partnered or cohabiting couple with or without children, or a lone parent with at least one child.'*

*** *'At least occasionally' includes those who answered 'occasionally', 'more often than not', 'most of the time' and 'all of the time'.*

25 May 2016

⇨ The above information is reprinted with kind permission from Relate. Please visit www.relate.org.uk for further information.

The nine most common reasons couples get divorced

Relationship counsellor Peter Saddington explains some of the reasons more than four in ten marriages fail.

By Elsa Vulliamy

Statistics show 42 per cent of marriages end in divorce, and 34 per cent of married couples divorce before their 20th wedding anniversary.

However, a study from Relate found 87 per cent of couples said they were in a good relationship, and that half rarely or never argued.

The statistics show that many couples who were previously in good relationships end up getting divorced within 20 years of their nuptials.

Relate counsellor and sex therapist Peter Saddington has given the nine most common reasons for divorce he sees in couples.

1. Money problems

Problems can arise when it comes to money if husband and wife have different value bases; for instance, if one person likes spending money freely and the other is more frugal and prefers saving.

2. Affairs

If one person is having an affair, this is likely to break down trust and lead to difficulties in establishing honesty in a relationship.

3. Interfering ex-partners

When establishing a new relationship, an ex getting your partner's attention can create tension.

It can feel like they're still married to the ex, or that the ex is more important.

4. Differences in sexual libido

It's a stereotype but not far off the mark. Many men want more sex than women and if couples have different levels of sexual libido this will lead to problems in the relationship.

5. Children from previous relationships

There is a big difference between how people react to their own children

and how they react to children they have become parent to. Parents make different allowances for children who are their own. When they are somebody else's children, it may be more difficult to establish the same relationship.

6. Intrusive parents

If parents are interfering, or if a partner perceives them to be, this can be a problem.

If one partner spends too much time talking with their mother, for example, this can create a breakdown of intimacy in the relationship.

7. Difference in how you resolve conflict

If someone has grown up in a family where arguing is very common and they're in a relationship with someone who doesn't like arguing or isn't used to it, this can cause difficulty.

Since you have different ways of solving problems, it's likely that these problems will never get resolved.

8. Differences in communication

If one partner is the type of person who shares all their intimate thoughts, but their partner is not, this can cause problems.

If one partner isn't sharing with the other, this will often be interpreted by the other as meaning "they don't love me, they're not interested in me".

9. Privacy problems

Another problem can be when one person has a different view of what should be kept within the relationship.

If one person shares all the intimate details of the relationship with their friends or over Facebook, this can be an increasingly difficult thing to manage.

16 February 2016

⇨ The above information is reprinted with kind permission from *The Independent*. Please visit www.independent.co.uk for further information.

© independent.co.uk 2017

Divorce can be nobody's fault – the law should do more to recognise that

An article from The Conversation.

By Sharon Thompson, Lecturer in Law, Cardiff University

THE CONVERSATION

The law affecting families in England and Wales is changing. Since legal aid was withdrawn in family law cases by legislation in 2012, resolving disputes amicably on divorce has never been more important. People are having to navigate a complex legal framework without legal support at the most emotionally fraught time of their lives.

But the law itself is failing divorcing couples by making compromise more difficult. It effectively encourages spouses to attribute blame even when no-one is at fault. Family lawyers and leading judges are now calling for legislative reform.

Since the 1970s, the sole ground for divorce in England and Wales is irretrievable breakdown of the marriage. This is established on proof of one of five facts: adultery, behaviour, desertion, two years separation with consent or five years separation without consent. The latter two facts require no fault but do mean years of waiting – and if a couple mutually wish to divorce there may be various emotional and economic reasons why they cannot wait this long.

So, although couples are not required to attribute blame to establish irretrievable breakdown, they are often compelled to do so if they want to end their marriage quickly. For instance, if one can prove that their spouse is guilty of adultery – an option not available to same-sex married couples – or behaviour that is unreasonable, the divorce can be finalised in less than six months. All this means that divorce is a much quicker process when there is someone to blame.

It is therefore unsurprising that the latest available statistics indicate that the most common reason spouses divorce is unreasonable behaviour. A YouGov survey commissioned in 2015 by Resolution, an organisation of family lawyers, found that 27% of couples proved irretrievable breakdown on the basis of fault because it was quicker and easier, admitting that neither spouse was to blame for the separation.

Fabricating fault

One of the most significant reasons spouses turn to apportioning blame is that their property and finances cannot be divided until the divorce is finalised. For individuals who had previously been financially dependent on their ex-partner, a delay of a couple of years in financial relief could be disastrous. One way of avoiding this is to blame the other party for the marriage breakdown, even if such allegations are untrue.

This is problematic to say the least. Spouses may ruin an otherwise amicable separation by having to decide whose name will be recorded on the divorce petition as being responsible for the end of the marriage. Worse still, this process is unnecessary, as allegations of fault in a divorce petition have no bearing on how the marital assets are subsequently divided.

Research has shown that this emphasis on fault increases animosity during relationship breakdown, because it encourages family disputes to be resolved in an adversarial way. The consequences of this are serious. Attributing blame can lead to bitterness and hostility, reducing the chance of reconciliation and prolonging the resolution of issues such as child arrangements and financial redistribution. It also costs more and puts pressure on court resources.

Not only is this detrimental to any children involved, but an emphasis on apportioning fault in proceedings could also jeopardise couples' chances for successful mediation. It has consistently been proven that mediation is less likely to be successful in high-conflict situations, yet fault-based divorce brings conflict to the fore. For the increasing numbers of people representing themselves in court, a fault-driven divorce process further aggravates an already volatile situation. This can be very damaging when there is no solicitor present to alleviate tensions.

Appetite for reform

Reform that eliminates fault from divorce law would not only encourage a non-adversarial process, but as president of the Family Division James Munby put it, more "intellectual honesty" would be brought to the divorce process because spouses would not have to make fictitious accusations of unreasonable behaviour against each other.

Calls for reform have been around for 20 years. The Law Commission recommended reform in 1990. But, provisions seeking to eliminate fault on divorce in the Family Law Act 1996 were never introduced and were repealed by the Children and Families Act 2014.

Now, amid recent developments such as the potential introduction of online divorce next year, reform may finally be imminent.

On 30 November, more than 150 family law practitioners from Resolution lobbied parliament to make divorce a "kinder process" by reducing the wait in cases where both spouses consent and no-one is deemed at fault from two years of separation to six months. There is also public appetite for no-fault divorce.

Those opposed to reform are concerned that it would mean a huge surge in the number of divorces, and that this, in turn, would destabilise the family unit. Yet, there is no research to support this and the divorce rate is currently at its lowest since the 1970s. In Scotland, where couples can consent to divorce after one year of separation without blaming either person, divorce rates are also decreasing.

Resolution's campaign for the removal of fault-based divorce highlights the pressing problems with divorce law in England and Wales. Fictional allegations of fault are exacerbating bitterness at a time when spouses must go increasingly through to the divorce proceedings without any legal support.

12 December 2016

⇨ The above information is reprinted with kind permission from *The Conversation*. Please visit www.theconversation.com for further information.

MPs need to get behind no-fault divorce if they're serious about reducing family conflict

Tomorrow (4 December) MPs are due to debate the introduction of no fault divorce, as Richard Bacon MP's No Fault Divorce Bill has its second reading. Leading family law organisation Resolution is urging MPs to support the principle of no fault divorce if they are serious about reducing family conflict and the ongoing impact of divorce.

Resolution chair Jo Edwards says:

"We know that our current fault-based divorce system achieves nothing besides escalating conflict during divorce. It does not act as a deterrent, nor does it help couples to salvage their marriage. The latest data from the Office of National Statistics shows that 114,720 people divorced in England and Wales in 2013, despite fault-based petitions.

"We are pleased to see Richard Bacon's Bill having a second reading. If MPs are serious about reducing family conflict and the trauma that can be caused by divorce, I would urge them to support the Bill as a welcome step towards removing the requirement of fault from divorce.

"Removing the blame from divorce, as proposed in Richard Bacon's Bill, would help couples who both wish to bring their relationship to a dignified conclusion and move on with their lives without the need for accusatory mud-slinging. This outdated system needs urgent revision – a civilised society deserves a civilised divorce process."

Recent research published by Resolution shows that the fault-based nature of divorce in England and Wales, which requires one person to accuse the other of adultery or unreasonable behaviour to have their divorce granted within two years of marriage breakdown, is driving over a quarter (27%) of divorcing couples to make false allegations to the court.

Resolution's research, carried out by YouGov (June 2015), found that:

⇨ 52% of divorce petitions were fault-based alleging either unreasonable behaviour or adultery

⇨ 27% of divorcing couples who asserted blame in their divorce petition admitted the allegation of fault wasn't true, but was the easiest option.

Resolution has campaigned for many years for the introduction of no-fault divorce, which was provided for in the Family Law Act 1996 but never implemented. Resolution has produced a briefing on no-fault divorce which has been sent to MPs ahead of tomorrow's debate.

Resolution's *Manifesto for Family Law*, endorsed by leading relationship and legal organisations including Relate, One Plus One, Only Dads and the Family Law Bar Association, calls for the removal of blame from the divorce process, bringing England and Wales into line with other modern jurisdictions including the United States, Australia and Spain.

3 December 2015

⇨ The above information is reprinted with kind permission from Resolution. Please visit www.resolution.org.uk for further information.

Digital divorce – how soon?

Today's *Times* ran a piece, "Online divorces to spare couples time and trouble" reporting that couples will be able to divorce online this year under plans that could open the way for the abolition of fault-based grounds for ending marriage.

The piece states that ministers are preparing a pilot project to allow divorce proceedings to be issued digitally for the first time, in a move to save time, paperwork and stress for thousands of people. More than 110,000 divorce proceedings were begun in 2015. It goes on to say that the plan, backed by England's most senior family judge, Sir James Munby, will be tested before being introduced across England and Wales in June.

So, paperless centralised online divorce will be available within six months in England and Wales then? Not so fast.

The summary of reforms in last September's Ministry of Justice (MoJ) consultation paper, 'Transforming our justice system' said that work had already begun by then to allow divorce applications to be made and managed online. It expressed the aim of removing some of the bureaucracy from often stressful and lengthy proceedings and simplifying cumbersome administrative processes.

The Court Service has now indeed begun to look at how it can build and roll out an online system and a small pilot is expected to commence shortly. However, HM Courts & Tribunals Service is not publicly committing to any date for when a full online system will be available to the general public.

Our enquiries have revealed that research has been carried out with "end users", divorcing spouses, about how any problems with the present procedure can be best tackled. This includes working with a specialist accessibility centre to help ensure the service is compliant and accessible for users who need additional features to allow them to access the service, such as using screen readers.

Family law solicitor and arbitrator, Tony Roe, who made a series of Freedom of Information requests of the MoJ, and whose research broke the news that Bury St Edmunds (BSE) would be the single divorce centre for London and the South East, has spoken to HMCTS in the light of *The Times'* story.

Roe said:

"It would be wrong to think that a complete digitalised divorce process will happen any time soon. At best only the petition may be available to complete online by the end of the summer, possibly. The Government's 'agile methodology' approach to projects apparently means that new processes are built bit by bit, starting with the petition in this case. It seems that family modernisation is leading the way being one of a small number of similar digital projects involving, for example, probate and tribunals.

It has been decided that there should be a pilot site and an announcement on this will be made very shortly. However, any such pilot will require minor rule changes via a Practice Direction (PD). As yet (3 January), no such PD has been published.

Excitement and expectation is growing in the family law community but we need to be patient and await the modernisation programme which seems likely to occur step by step, starting with a likely pilot, a PD and only then the first digital petition.'

3 January 2017

⇨ The above information is reprinted with kind permission from LexisNexis. Please visit www.familylaw.co.uk for further information.

Tips for a stress-free divorce

Divorce can cause problems such as stress, anxiety, depression and panic attacks according to Paula Hall, relationship psychotherapist at the charity Relate.

"This can affect sleep, which can cause tiredness, exhaustion and a lack of focus and concentration," she says.

"There's a lot to think about during a divorce, particularly looking after children, telling your parents and dealing with their emotions, moving house, dividing possessions, setting up bank accounts, and continuing your job."

Below, Paula identifies seven crucial steps for coping.

1. Accept the reality of your situation

Ask yourself questions about what happened and try to understand what went on beneath the surface. For example, if the other person had an affair, try to understand what led them to do that. Similarly, if you grew apart, think about how you've changed since you first met.

2. Manage your emotions

The most common emotions people experience during a divorce are grief, fear, anger, resentment, doubt, regret and guilt. At this early stage in particular you need help and support from friends. You also need to give yourself time and space. Some techniques of cognitive behavioural therapy (CBT) can really help, such as changing negative thoughts and learning how to be optimistic.

3. Develop strategies for personal growth

Recognise your strengths and your weaknesses, and develop an action plan. An action plan involves setting goals. For example, if you know you'll struggle with loneliness, decide how you will deal with this. This will build your self-esteem and help you manage your feelings, such as missing someone.

4. Let friends and family help

Identify your support network. Think about the people who are already there for you. But also recognise that some relationships may be challenging, such as friends who will be hard to socialise with or a family member who might say:

"I told you it'd never work." Think about the relationships you want to strengthen. If you're fairly good friends with someone you work with, see them more often. Or maybe you could renew contact with someone who has been through a divorce.

5. Deal with money and practical matters

Think about your financial and practical resources and challenges. This might include how to release some of the equity in your house, or how you can make money during the free time you now have. It may also include things as simple as learning how to use a lawnmower or the washing machine, or how to cook for the children when they're staying with you. It's often these practical things that make people feel like they can't cope.

6. Communicate effectively with your ex

This is another area that can cause a huge amount of stress. If you have children, learning to communicate effectively is very important. This involves trying not to get angry, managing your emotions, and entering into conversations with a clear idea of what you want to achieve without getting drawn into old arguments.

You may want to consider family mediation. This helps people facing relationship breakdown sort out practical issues, such as arrangements for their children and sorting out their finances.

Family mediation services charge for their services, but you may be able to get legal aid if you are on a low income.

Find a family mediation service near you.

7. Set goals for the future

It's important to adopt the belief that "today is the first day of the rest of your life". This could mean being single, being satisfied, dating and finding love again, as well as realising your hopes, dreams and ambitions.

"Divorce can be devastating and painful, and there will be bad days," says Paula. "But negative thinking leads to negative emotions, which lead to bad health, so it's important to try to think positively."

Paula is keen to stress the potential for a positive outcome. She says: "Divorce is an opportunity for change. There are lots of things you can't do if you're married. People compromise and put things to one side, such as hobbies or even careers. A divorce is an opportunity to think about the things you loved but might have let go of, while recognising that you can reshape your future."

25 March 2015

⇨ The above information is reprinted with kind permission from NHS Choices. Please visit www.nhs.uk for further information.

© NHS Choices 2017

Parents who share family time at meals are less likely to get divorced

Parents who share family time during meals – without the TV on – are less likely to get divorced.

Divorce risk is less in families who eat together – but only if the TV isn't switched on.

Researchers have found that families who spend 30 more minutes per day than other families in family mealtimes have a 30% less risk of parental separation – but only if the TV isn't on during the meal.

The study of 5,604 families looked at a host of other factors that might be connected with the chances of parental separation, but didn't find any links. Having the TV on at mealtimes removed the positive association between family mealtimes and family stability.

Just as interesting were factors that weren't conducive to a reduction in the chance of separation; they included religious observance and the time that fathers spend alone with their children.

Poor relationship quality, of course, is a strong predictor of separation, but when the researchers controlled for relationship quality, family mealtimes with the TV off stood out.

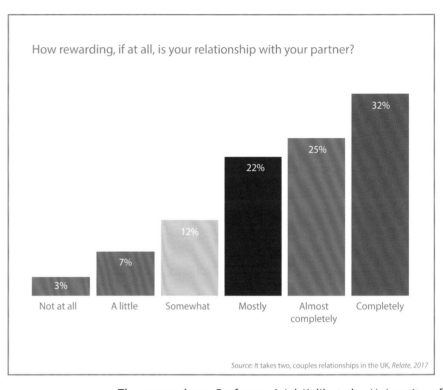

How rewarding, if at all, is your relationship with your partner?

- Not at all: 3%
- A little: 7%
- Somewhat: 12%
- Mostly: 22%
- Almost completely: 25%
- Completely: 32%

Source: It takes two, couples relationships in the UK, Relate, 2017

The researchers, Professor Ariel Kalil at the University of Chicago and Mari Rege at the University of Stavanger in Norway, explored what might connect mealtimes without TV to a reduction in the chances of family separation.

Evidence suggests that when families share mealtimes with conversation, mothers are more positive about marital quality and happier with the relationship. Perhaps the key is the opportunity for communication that mealtimes afford, provided the TV is off.

Further reading

Kalil A & Rege M, We Are Family: Fathers' Time with Children and the Risk of Parental Relationship Dissolution, Social Forces (2015) doi:10.1093/sf/sov076

24 May 2016

⇨ The above information is reprinted with kind permission from the Child & Family Blog. Please visit www. childandfamilyblog.com for further information.

It's dinner time! What are you doing?

Improving our family relationship!

Help for children and young adults

If your mum and dad are separating or getting a divorce, you may be feeling very sad. You may also be feeling:

⇨ angry

⇨ confused

⇨ worried.

Whatever you are feeling, that's OK. Everyone feels different and there is no right or wrong way to feel.

You may be wondering what will happen in the future:

⇨ Where will I live?

⇨ Will I still see mum and dad?

⇨ Why can't they still love each other?

You will probably have lots of questions but might not be sure if it's okay to talk about your worries to your mum and dad. If you'd prefer to someone different, why not contact ChildLine?

ChildLine is a counselling service for children and young people. You can contact ChildLine about anything – no problem is too big or too small. If you are feeling scared or out of control or just want to talk to someone you can contact ChildLine.

A ChildLine counsellor is someone:

⇨ Who will believe you and knows it takes courage to contact them

⇨ Who you can trust

⇨ Who won't judge you or put you down

⇨ Who is not easily shocked

⇨ Who understands the sorts of problems you might be worried about

⇨ Who is trained to help.

You don't have to give your name or any details about yourself if you don't want to.

You can contact ChildLine about anything, so think about how you feel and tell them about it. The more you tell them about what is happening and how it makes you feel, the more they can understand and help you. They might ask you some questions to try and understand how you are feeling or to help you talk about it. You don't have to answer them if you don't want to. You can get back in touch at anytime, even if you didn't tell them anything the first time you contacted them.

Family separation brings a lot of changes. There are a number of websites that will help you to understand what may happen and how to cope.

It's not your fault

This website has lots of useful information that will help you cope. Including what you might be feeling, how to feel better and how your mum and dad can help you.

Cafcass (Children and Family Court Advisory and Support)

If your parents are going to court because they can't agree on who will look after you, this website will help you to understand how things will work. Cafcass looks after the interests of children in family courts.

CyberMentors

CyberMentors is all about young people helping and supporting each other online. If you're being bullied, or are feeling a bit low, or are maybe troubled by something and you're not sure what to do or who to talk to, then CyberMentors is where you can go for help. It doesn't matter how big or small you think the problem is, or whether you're being targeted online or offline, CyberMentors are here to listen and support you.

CBBC Newsround

"My parents split up last year, it started when I was four, I was really scared but now I am fine with it because I know it wasn't my fault and that both my parents love me." Views about splitting up from children themselves.

⇨ The above information is reprinted with kind permission from The Centre for Separated Families. Please visit www.separatedfamilies.info for further information.

© The Centre for Separated Families 2017

My parents are separating: young people's experiences

Ellie's story

Ellie (1), member of the Family Justice Young People's Board, shares her experience of her parents' breakdown and how Cafcass helped when her parents went to court.

"It was a few years ago and it was hard for me and my brother. The whole thing was scary because we didn't know what was happening or what was going to happen. Also, when you're a kid the only thing you know about courts is that it's a place for criminals, and that made it scary too. Why were we going to court? That's not a place where we should go. Everything felt really unstable.

"Cafcass set up a meeting to explain what was going on and that helped. They told us why we were going through this process. It was useful to have them break down the situation and explain what was going on. I didn't feel so scared after that.

"It was good to speak to the Cafcass worker because at that point it was really hard to talk to my parents, really hard to communicate with both of them. Cafcass told us about the possible outcomes and what might happen, and that was helpful.

"Me and my brother were really happy with the outcome. I live with my mum now, but I see my dad nearly every day. He doesn't live far from me. My mum and dad are on speaking terms now as well, which is really good.

"I would say to any young person going through this, don't be afraid to say how you're feeling and don't be afraid to ask questions if you don't understand something. It's better to ask there and then because you have to go through the whole process and there's a big decision that's going to be made at the end of the day and you have to know what's going on so you can tell people how you feel.

"One thing that changed after the process was that I'm actually closer to my dad now. He was always the stricter parent, so when I said I wanted to live with my mum, I was scared to tell him, but he was okay with it and asked me when I wanted to see him. He reassured me and now I feel like I can talk to him about anything because I could tell him that and it was okay.

"I'm really excited to be on the Young People's Board. I think it's so important that young people who have actually been through this can help determine how things can change and how the process works at Cafcass. It's a really good set up that young people can have their say."

(1) Name has been changed.

Jason's story

"Hello. My name's Jason. I am seven years old.

"Last year my mum and dad were shouting all the time, and one day my dad stormed off.

"I was really sad when dad left, and I didn't really understand what was happening. My mum was upset too, and one day dad came round but mum wouldn't let him in. I still wanted to see my dad, but I didn't like telling my mum because she got upset.

"After a while, my mum told me that someone would come and talk to me about what was happening. Her name was Anne, and she said she was from Cafcass. Anne talked to me about my mum and dad, and then she came with me to see dad in a special room called a contact centre. It had toys that I could play with. I played with dad for a while on the table football, and Anne was watching. I had a nice time and I liked seeing dad again. Anne also came to see me at home, and talked to my mum there as well.

"I told Anne that I liked playing with my dad, and I missed him. But it was better at home now there was no shouting and arguing.

"Anne said that she was going to write a report for the court about me and my family, and about spending time with my mum and dad. I thought she was going to ask me who I wanted to live with, but she didn't. We talked about my pets and school, and drew some pictures about dad and mum. Anne told me that someone called a judge would decide about me seeing mum and dad, but they wanted to know what I thought. I didn't say much about this, and Anne said that was OK.

"My mum and dad went to the family court, and the judge listened to everyone, and read Anne's report. The judge then made a decision about seeing my dad, and mum told me what they had decided."

Kelly's story

"Hi! My name's Kelly. I was 11 when my mum and dad split up. There was a big row and dad left, and my younger brother Darren and I stayed with our mum.

"At first I did not really know what was happening. I was worried because my mum was so angry and upset, but I also missed dad. I heard my mum on the phone talking to a solicitor so I thought something might be happening in court. I wanted to ask about dad and granny who we used to see every Saturday, but I thought mum might get upset.

"A man from Cafcass called Jim came to meet me and Darren. I was a bit nervous as I thought he would ask me lots of questions. However, he seemed to understand what it was like for children when their mums and dads split up. Jim said he was going to talk to us and write a report for the court to help them decide what to do. He arranged to meet me and Darren in his office as that was a private place to talk. Darren liked it there because there were lots of good toys, and I found it easier to talk to him than I thought it would be.

"I told Jim that I knew mum and dad were very angry with each other and that I didn't want to see any more rows between them. I also told her I missed my granny a lot and her dog Spotty which we used to take for walks every weekend.

"Jim sorted it out so that Darren and I could start visiting dad at granny's house. I liked this better than seeing my dad in his new flat as it felt strange there, and I didn't really know his new girlfriend. Jim also helped explain to mum that I didn't like her saying mean things about dad.

"After a few weeks Jim came back and talked through what she was putting in her report for the court. I was worried about mum and dad being cross about what I had told him, so Jim helped me sort out exactly what I wanted to say to them. He said that he would suggest to the court that Darren and I live with mum but see dad and granny every weekend.

"At the family court, the Judge listened to everyone, and read Jim's report, and then made a decision about where Darren and I should live."

PS from Darren

"I did not really know what was happening. I thought my dad was working away from home and would come back although I heard him shout at my mum a lot and that scared me. Jim was nice although I did not fancy going to his office. I thought it would be lots of boring talking. But there were good toys. Jim did not make me say a lot. I was glad I had Kelly with me. Jim had met my granny and knew we liked going to her house at weekends. Now we go and see dad, granny and Spotty every week."

⇨ The above information is reprinted with kind permission from Cafcass. Please visit www.cafcass.gov.uk for further information.

⇨ Please note that Cafcass only become involved in about 10% of all parental separation cases.

"What should I have done differently?" A conversation with my son about divorce

Sixteen years later, Suzanne Finnamore's son Pablo tells her how his parents' split looked from a child's perspective: "It was like being a double agent."

Sixteen years ago, my first husband sallied out the door toward his new life with another woman and a baby on the way. "You'll get the papers next week," he said, the automatic window of his SUV sliding up as he roared off. Meanwhile, there was already a baby at our house. His name was Pablo. "Oh my God," I thought. "How will we get through this without a husband and a father? Will our son grow up angry? Will he be devastated? Resentful?"

Nearly two decades later, Pablo isn't psychologically maimed, or plotting his revenge against us as I'd originally feared. In fact, he's just fine.

He was a baby when we split, and then a boy, and young boys don't talk much about feelings. I never really knew all of what went on in his curly-haired head. Now that he's 18, it feels like the right time for us to talk about the divorce – what I did right, what I did wrong, and what he wished I knew. I hope this conversation can be a guide to parents in the midst of ending their marriage, mothers and fathers wondering how their kids will fare.

Did you have any sense that things were coming to an end between your father and me?

Pablo: As a toddler, I barely had a sense of how day turned to night or where the Teletubbies went when the TV turned off. So no. I was blissfully unaware. Just growing teeth.

And filling diapers. I always felt that the fact that you didn't potty train until you were four was your way of wresting control. Like, I can't control anything but I can crap my pants. Without a husband to help me and with a hectic work schedule, I learned to improvise. I learned to do what I called the Standing Change, wherein I changed your

diaper while you stood up, in about ten seconds flat. Was there a moment when it hit you that we were different from other families?

I felt no emptiness at the table, no lack of father in the living room. There was never a moment where I felt like our house was wrong. But the first time I had to get on a plane, at age five, to see my dad in Los Angeles, it hit me. I was distracted by the pilot and the fawning flight attendants but looking out the window, it felt like a lot. I had to enter the stratosphere just to see my dad.

I put you on that airplane and I was fine; your flight was less than an hour long. I was almost relieved: a whole weekend to myself. Then I burst into tears. It was like my heart had been placed in ice and ferried away. I'd spent time without you before on weekends while you were at your grandparents', but this was different. This was you flying away into the sky. I came unglued, shambling to my car like some blithering zombie, saying your name over and over to myself, like a mantra. When did you feel the effects of our divorce most acutely?

I remember I was seven or eight and I heard some Luther Vandross song about dancing with his father. I was shocked when I began to cry. For years, I'd kept most of my emotions hidden. But somehow all of that changed with a simple R&B song. The line "My father would lift me high… and I knew for sure I was loved" resonated strongly with me. I didn't have the kind of memories he sang about. I had lost them.

Yes. I couldn't listen to passionate love songs or watch sitcoms where there was a funny dad just bumbling around, just taken for granted. They

made me feel I'd lost something important that everyone else had. Instead I focused on Dr Phil and CNN, especially reports about natural disasters. That seemed more relevant. Watching and rewatching all the plane crashes on *Seconds From Disaster* was oddly comforting to me. But that's how I manage things. I go toward the wreckage. I examine it. **How do feel about the way your dad and I handled the divorce?**

Your divorce was laid with a calm presence. "Your father left me, not you," is what I remember you emphasising. You always encouraged me to see him when I could.

He took me to restaurants and movies, subtly revealing the things men should like (Dijon mustard; Halle Berry; a simple brown baseball cap was "a hat with guts"). I came to see my dad as one might view a loving uncle who visits pretty often. I picked up on you two acting like friends for my sake, but didn't mind.

Indeed. We both refrained from venting our spleens in front of you. Because it would splatter you. Plus, your father is half of you; that's a biological fact. I can't condemn that half. Still, it was horrifying when

it all came crashing down like a cheap house of cards. I wanted to die, which was out of the question because I had you. I had you and that saved me. **What was the worst part for you?**

A lot of kids with divorced parents feel like pawns in an ongoing skirmish to see who is the better parent. I usually didn't feel this way. But I do remember being put on the phone with my father while you argued. You were driving me to school and begging him to visit. You passed the phone to me and told me to say how much I missed him, and thrust your argument into my hands.

I also want to say my father is a man I deeply love, who is irreplaceable, who I've taken and accepted despite his leaving, who calls whether I pick up or not. I need to say that before I say he has also acted like a careless runaway. Having to be in the middle of it, to request a visit I hardly wanted and to hear shame in his voice, that was the worst part.

Wow. I come off really bad in this, as does he. I know he missed you dreadfully. Sometimes I would waive child support so he could buy a ticket to come see you, as he moved from one distant place to another more distant place. It was

like some hideous game of keep-away. **What do you wish I had done differently?**

Nothing. If a Freudian analyst had been around, he might have jotted down: "Mother projects anger toward ex-husband on to son" – but, I don't know. I'm trying to think of a lastingly hurtful choice you made. But all that's coming to mind is you making me tacos, the smell of the sizzling beef. You used to roll me up in a blanket and call me burrito boy, pretending to sprinkle cheese on me. That's all I can think of.

There are definitely things I'd have done differently. I wouldn't have started secretly smoking that first year, because I am a bad smoker and late at night a lot of nice comforters were ruined. I would have started dating sooner. Five years was too long. But I had you to raise, and I got to have every minute of that, unadulterated. What was the most challenging part for you?

Not hurting either of you. Like, I couldn't just say to my father that I didn't miss him so much, because I loved him too. And I couldn't tell you I'd begun turning to him to discuss things that were too uncomfortable to talk over with you. It was sort of like being a double agent.

This conversation has been a revelation. As a mother, seeing how you turned out is all that matters to me. I literally can't imagine my life without the divorce. While it was harrowing and painful, I also feel like it was a lucky break, a kind of drastic intervention that saved us.

Suzanne Finnamore is the bestselling author of *Split: A Memoir of Divorce*. Her forthcoming novel, *The Ghost Husband*, is deep in the works. Pablo Finnamore is studying English literature at North Carolina State University in Raleigh. He also writes poetry.

13 October 2016

⇨ The above information is reprinted with kind permission from *The Guardian*. Please visit www.theguardian.com for further information.

Key facts

- The vast majority of people enjoy good quality relationships: 87% of people in couples are happy with their relationships; 71% of us enjoy good relationships with our colleagues; and nine out of ten of us report having close friends. (page 1)

- 61% of parents identifying money worries as a top strain on relationships; 22% of workers saying they work more hours than they want to and this damages their health; and one in six people who are disabled or living with long-term health conditions reporting that they have no close friends. (page 1)

- Recent research from Marriage Foundation has also showed that marriage is increasingly the preserve of the rich. Among UK parents with children under five, 87% of those in the top income quintile were married compared to 24% in the bottom quintile. (page 2)

- On average, 82% of parents in the highest income quintile are married compared to 42% of parents in the lowest income quintile. (page 2)

- The highest marriage gap overall is found in Denmark, where 81% of the richest parents are married, 3.9 times the level of 26% among the poorest parents. (page 2)

- You can get married or form a civil partnership in the UK if you're:
  - 16 or over
  - free to marry or form a civil partnership (single, divorced or widowed)
  - not closely related. (page 3)

- The number of humanist weddings performed in Scotland has grown exponentially since their legal recognition as marriages, reversing the overall decline in the number of marriages in Scotland. In 2010 Humanist Society Scotland (HSS) performed more marriages than the Catholic Church, and in 2013 it performed more than double. (page 6)

- Same-sex couples are not permitted to marry in any of the 17,350 churches of the Church of England and the Church in Wales, or in nearly 23,000 other places of worship, such as Roman Catholic churches, Islamic mosques, and Hindu temples. (page 11)

- Only 139 places of worship are registered to perform same-sex marriage in England and Wales, meaning approximately 99.5 per cent do not offer it. (page 11)

- Of 12 wedding traditions surveyed by YouGov, seven traditions were still favoured by more than half of people. The most popular wedding traditions are the groom having a best man (78%), the bride and groom's first dance (75%) and the best man's speech (73%). (page 13)

- Half (51%) of cohabitees think government benefits are biased in favour of married couples. (page 17)

- A third (33%) of cohabitees have not yet named the beneficiary of their pension. (page 17)

- Cohabitees' finances are in poorer health than married couples, with lower incomes and less savings. (page 17)

- Three quarters (74%) of cohabitees do not have a will and 64% have no life insurance. (page 17)

- One in ten (10%) cohabitees also admit to only being with their partner as they cannot afford to separate. (page 17)

- The US has the sixth highest divorce rate of any country, with 3.6 annual divorces per 1,000 inhabitants, according to the most recent figures available. (page 24)

- Three in five British children (62%) born to unmarried couples experience family breakdown before they hit their teen years. (page 25)

- In 2015, a YouGov poll found that as many as 61 per cent of Britons have stayed in an unhappy relationship for much longer than they think they should have. Only six per cent of the more than 2,000 people surveyed claimed they had broken up with their partner soon after realising they were not a good match. (page 27)

- A staggering 2.87 million people across the UK are living in relationships which would be described within clinical practice as distressed, according a new study by Relate, the UK's leading relationships charity. This equates to 18% of married or cohabiting couples and 1.4 million UK families. (page 29)

- Statistics show 42 per cent of marriages end in divorce, and 34 per cent of married couples divorce before their 20th wedding anniversary. (page 30)

- Researchers have found that families who spend 30 more minutes per day than other families in family mealtimes have a 30% less risk of parental separation – but only if the TV isn't on during the meal. (page 35)

Arranged marriage

A marriage that is arranged by the parents of the bride and groom. Arranged marriage is very different from forced marriage, because the bride and groom agree to the process.

Bigamy

Marrying more than one person. This is a criminal offence, punishable by law.

Child marriage

Where children, often before they have reached puberty, are given to be married – often to a person many years older.

Civil partnership

The Civil Partnership Act 2004 (CPA) allowed LGB people the right to form legal partnerships for the first time, giving them rights comparable to those of married couples. A civil partnership is a new legal relationship, exclusively for same-sex couples, distinct from marriage.

Cohabitation

People in an intimate relationship who live together. In the eyes of the law, cohabiting couples do not have the same rights as married couples (for example, a couple who are cohabiting do not qualify to be each others' next of kin).

Common law marriage

Many people believe that a marriage-like relationship can be established simply by cohabiting for an extended period of time. In legal terms, this is not true. Cohabitation does not lead to the same rights as marriage.

Divorce

The legal separation of husband and wife.

Forced marriage

A marriage that takes place without the consent of one or both parties. Forced marriage is not the same as arranged marriage, which is organised by family or friends but which both parties freely enter into.

Living Together Agreement

A legal agreement, reached between cohabiting couples, which aims to clearly define what should happen in relation to property, assets and children should the couple break up.

Marriage

When a man and a woman join together in a close and intimate union that is recognised by law, becoming husband and wife. In the UK, the legal age at which you can marry is 18-years-old, or 16- to 17-years-old if you have parental consent.

Marriage (Same Sex Couples) Bill 2012–13

Currently, same-sex marriage is not permitted under UK law. The Same Sex Couples Bill aims to introduce civil marriage for same-sex couples in England and Wales. Some argue that same-sex marriage will 'weaken the institution of marriage', while others are strongly in favour of the Bill. The Same Sex Couples Bill would also allow homosexual couples to wed in religious ceremonies, if the registered buildings/premises agree.

Monogamy

Monogamous relationships involve just two partners.

Polygamy

Relationships that involve more than two people. For example, having more than one spouse.

Prenuptial agreement (pre-nup)

A contract entered into by the two people before they are married or enter into a civil union together. A prenuptial agreement functions as an insurance policy, detailing how assets would be divided in the case of a separation.

Assignments

Brainstorming

⇨ In small groups, discuss what you know about marriage in the UK.

  • What is the difference between marriage and civil partnership?

  • What is a humanist ceremony?

  • What are the options for same-sex couples who want to get married?

Research

⇨ Choose a religion and research its marriage traditions. Create a presentation that explains and demonstrates your chosen religion's marriage customs. Try using pictures, music or video to make your presentation exciting and engaging.

⇨ Research the British Humanist Association and create a presentation explaining their core principles and beliefs. Include information about Humanist wedding ceremonies.

⇨ Research marriage traditions in a country other than your own. Create a PowerPoint presentation to explore these traditions and share with your class.

⇨ Create a map of the world and colour code each country according to their laws surrounding same-sex marriage.

Design

⇨ Choose one of the articles from this book and create an illustration that highlights the key themes of the piece.

⇨ Design a leaflet that explains the legal rights of cohabiting couples.

⇨ Design a poster that illustrates five of the most popular wedding traditions in the UK.

⇨ Design a website containing advice and information for parents who are struggling to talk to their children about the issue of divorce. You could use the articles on pages 36, 37 and 38 for inspiration about the kinds of things that might be useful.

⇨ Create a campaign that will raise awareness of the issue of child marriage. Your campaign could take the form of television ads, banners that would appear on social networking sites such as Facebook, or even posters on the London Underground network. Produce a campaign plan and samples.

Oral

⇨ "Pre-nuptual agreements are only necessary for rich people." Debate this statement as a class, with half of you arguing in agreement and half arguing against.

⇨ In small groups, discuss whether you think couples should be allowed to have a church wedding if they do not have any religious beliefs. Why do you think people who aren't religious want to be married in church? Make notes on your discussion and share with the rest of your class.

⇨ In small groups, discuss the difference between forced marriage and arranged marriage.

⇨ Divide into small groups and script a radio show in which the host is asking listeners 'What is the point of getting married? Why not just live together instead?' One member of your group should play the part of the radio host and the others should call-in to voice their opinions.

Reading/writing

⇨ Write a one-paragraph definition of the word 'marriage' and then compare it with a classmate's.

⇨ Read the article *Europe's marriage gap between rich and poor* on page two and write a summary for your local paper.

⇨ Read the article *"Some people don't like the phrase man and wife"*... on page eight and write a bullet point summary of the author's key points.

⇨ Write a blog post exploring whether you believe humanist weddings should be legally binding in England, as they are in Scotland.

⇨ In pairs, imagine you are in a long-term relationship and draft a Living Together Agreement. Think carefully about the kinds of things you would include and how best to approach them without hurting your partner's feelings.

⇨ Write a blog post explaining the difference between civil partnership and same-sex marriage. In your post, you should also consider whether civil partnership should be offered to heterosexual couples as well as homosexual couples.

⇨ Write a blog post arguing in favour of 'no-fault divorce'.

Acknowledgements

The publisher is grateful for permission to reproduce the material in this book. While every care has been taken to trace and acknowledge copyright, the publisher tenders its apology for any accidental infringement or where copyright has proved untraceable. The publisher would be pleased to come to a suitable arrangement in any such case with the rightful owner.

Images

All images courtesy of iStock except page 24 © Chris Lawton, page 26 © Cara Acred, page 28 © Cloud Visual, page 33 © Alejandro Escamilla and page 39 © Jordan Whitt.

Icons

Icons on page 41 was made by Freepik from www.flaticon.com.

Illustrations

Don Hatcher: pages 18 & 35. Simon Kneebone: pages 7 & 27. Angelo Madrid: pages 2 & 21.

Additional acknowledgements

Editorial on behalf of Independence Educational Publishers by Cara Acred.

With thanks to the Independence team: Mary Chapman, Sandra Dennis, Jackie Staines and Jan Sunderland.

Cara Acred

Cambridge, May 2017